AN TÁIN BÓ CÚALGNE
DEIRDRE

THE MACMILLAN COMPANY
NEW YORK · BOSTON · CHICAGO · DALLAS
ATLANTA · SAN FRANCISCO

MACMILLAN & CO., LIMITED
LONDON · BOMBAY · CALCUTTA
MELBOURNE

THE MACMILLAN CO. OF CANADA, LTD.
TORONTO

DEIRDRE

BY

JAMES STEPHENS

New York
THE MACMILLAN COMPANY
1923

Copyright, 1923,
By THE MACMILLAN COMPANY.

Set up and electrotyped.   Published September, 1923,

THE FERRIS PRINTING COMPANY
NEW YORK

Do chum glóire Dé agus onóra na h-Eireann.

BOOK I

CHAPTER I

ONCE on a time Conachúr mac Nessa[1] was on a journey, and had to pass the night at the house of Felimid mac Dall, his story-teller. He was annoyed because his wife, Maeve, had not come with him, but Maeve had the knack of annoying him more than any one else was able to; so that when he thought of her his mind went intriguing and adventuring, for he was always trying to get the better of her, and was seldom without the feeling that she was getting or had just got the best of him.

For this reason he was irritable and could not look at any one with benevolence except Fergus mac Roy. But he could not look otherwise than benevolently on Fergus.

Meantime, night was at hand, and one

[1] Conachúr = pron. Kun-a-hoor; mac = pron. mock.

must sleep, and it is vexatious to sleep
alone.

He clapped his hands, and said to the
attendant who appeared:

"Is Felimid mac Dall married?"

"He is, master."

"Give my compliments to Felimid," said
Conachúr, "and tell him that his wife is to
sleep with me to-night."

The attendant vanished and the king was
left alone. That is, he was left to his
thoughts, for when he was among those he
was where other men might not care to
follow him. In fact, the large room wherein
he sat was almost uncomfortably filled with
men : but they kept respectfully apart, playing chess, and speaking in low voices to one
another.

The attendant returned.

"A Rí Uasal!" said he humbly.

"Well?" said Conachúr.

"The master of the house regrets that
his wife cannot sleep with you to-night."

"Here is something new," said the king
sternly.

"His wife is at this moment in childbed,"
murmured the discreet servant.

4

"These women are always troublesome," said the king with jovial anger. "She troubles me by withdrawing herself from my comfort, and she troubles my poor Felimid by giving him a child he could well do without."

He looked moodily on his gentlemen. There was Cathfa,[1] the famous poet, and Conall his grandson, to be known later as Cearnac (the victorious), but already notable; bitter-tongued Bricriu, who was famous or infamous according to one's judgement; Uisneac, who had married one of Cathfa's three daughters, and for whose little son Naoise the queens of Ireland would weep so long as Ireland had a memory; and there was Fergus mac Roy.

Conachúr's eye travelled loweringly from one to the other of these men until it rested on Fergus, and on him it rested lovingly, benevolently.

He looked loweringly on the others because they did not stand in any particular relation to him at the moment. He looked lovingly and mildly on Fergus because he hated Fergus and had wronged him so bitterly that he must wrong him yet more in

[1] Cathfa=pron. Kaffa.

5

justification. His wife and Fergus mac Roy
were often in his thoughts, so he looked very
lovingly on them and speculated a great deal
about their future.

But this night the young king was seri-
ously out of humour, not only because of his
wife's absence, but because of many things
that had happened. Three comets in succession had flashed across the sky as they drove
to the Story-teller's house. His leading
chariot-horse had trod in a rabbit-hole and
its leg was cracked at the fetlock; and one
of his attendants had been taken with mortal
vomitings, and it did not seem that he would
finish until he had emptied his body of his
soul.

Conachúr called to his father:

"You are a poet, and should be able to
tell us the meaning of these various omens."

"It is not hard to tell," said the calm
magician.

"Then tell it," quoth the king testily.

As he spoke a thin wail came from somewhere in the building, and the men present
turned an ear to that little sound, and then
a questioning or humorous eye on each
other.

6

"You hear," said the poet. "A child has just been born in this house. She will bring evil to Ireland, and she will work destruction in Ulster as a ferret works destruction in a rabbit's burrow."

Cathfa then returned to his chess, leaving the company staring.

"You have the gift of comfortable prophecy," said the king.

"Put an end to the prophecy by putting an end to the child," Bricriu advised, "and then let us see how the gods manage their affairs."

"Bricriu, my soul," said the king, "you like troubling the waters, but to-night you seem to be afflicted with sense. Bring the creature to me."

They carried the little morsel to him and she was laid across his knees.

"So you are to destroy my kingdom and bring evil to mighty Ireland?"

The babe reached with a tiny claw and gripped one finger of the king.

"See," he laughed, "she places herself under my protection," and he moved his finger to and fro, but the child held fast to it.

"Ulster is under your protection," growled Bricriu.

The king, who did not like other men's advice, looked at him.

"It is not soldierly, nor the act of a prince, to evade fate," said he who was to be known afterwards as the wide-eyed, majestic monarch. "Therefore, all that can happen will happen, and we shall bear all that is to be borne."

Then he gave the child back to its trembling nurse.

Cathfa looked up from the chess-board.

"She is to be called the 'Troubler,'" said he.

And from that day "Deirdre" was her name.

CHAPTER II

W<small>HEN</small> Echaid Yellow-Heel was King of Ulster, he had a daughter called Assa. She was educated apart from her father's residence by twelve tutors, and none of these had ever trained a pupil who was so docile, so teachable, or so affectionate. She loved knowledge, and so she loved learned men and would be always in their company.

One day she went on a visit to her father's court, and when she returned to her lessons she found that her twelve tutors had been murdered, and there was nothing to tell who had killed them.

From that moment her nature changed. She put on the dress of a female warrior, gathered a company about her, and went marauding and plundering in every direction. She was no longer called Assa (the Gentle),

9

but Nessa, or the Ungentle, was her name thenceforth.

Cathfa, the son of Ross, was then a young, powerful, and ambitious man, learning magic, or practising what he had learned, and it was he had slain the tutors, but Nessa did not know this. It may be that Cathfa had visited the tutors during her absence, and, for young magicians do not love argument, he may have killed them after a dispute.

Once, on one of her marauding expeditions, she went questing in a wilderness. At a distance there was a spring of clear water, and, while her people were preparing food, Nessa went to this spring to bathe. She was in the water when Cathfa passed, for he also was in that wilderness, and when he saw the girl's body he loved her, for she was young and lovely. He approached, and placed himself between the girl and her dress and weapons, and he held a sword over her head.

"Spare me," she pleaded.

"If you will be my wife I will spare you," said Cathfa.

She agreed to that, for no other course was open to her, and they rejoined her party.

They were married, and Nessa's father

gave them a bride-gift of land, called afterwards Rath Cathfa, in the country of the Picts in Crí Ross. In time a son was born to those two, namely, Conachúr mac Nessa, for it was by his mother's name he was known, and it was for him that Cathfa made the poem beginning :

Welcome to the stranger that has come here.

There are some who say, however, that Fachtna the Mighty had been the leman of Nessa, and that it was he was the father of Conachúr instead of Cathfa. If so, as Fachtna was the son of Maga, who was daughter of Anger mac an Og of the Brugh, then Conachúr had the blood of a god in his veins as well as the blood of a mortal, and much of his great success and of his terrible failure can be accounted for; for the gods are unlucky in love, so, too, the son of a wise mother is unlucky in love, as is also the man who is fortunate in war.

After some time Nessa left her husband, taking her son with her. It may be that she had discovered he was the murderer of her tutors. It may have been that she did not love him; it may even be that she did not like being wife to a magician, or he may have grown tired of her. But she never returned to him again.

But when Conachúr was a youth Nessa was still the most beautiful woman of Ulster. The then King of Ulster, Fachtna the Mighty, died, and his young half-brother, Fergus, the son of Roy, wife of Ross the Red, son of Rury, came to the throne. Fergus was then eighteen years of age and Conachúr was sixteen, and, like Conachúr, Fergus also was known by his mother's name instead of his father's.

Nessa came to the Ulster court with her son, and while there Fergus fell madly in love with her, and she could in no way avoid the importunities of that monstrous youth, for Fergus was gigantic in bulk and stature.

"I shall marry you on one condition," said Nessa.

"I agree to it beforehand," said Fergus.

"You know the great love I bear my son, Conachúr?"

"I also love him," said Fergus.

"His descent is kingly," she said, "and I desire that he should be a king if it were only for a year.   If you resign the crown to him during our first year of marriage I will marry you."

"I will do that," said Fergus.

That was done, and for a year Fergus and Nessa lived happily together.

But Nessa was not entirely absorbed in love.   She was still thinking of her son. During that year she arranged a marriage for Conachúr with Clothru, the daughter of the High King of Ireland, and she spent a vast treasure in working among the nobles and important people of Ulster, so that they became of her son's party as against the party of her husband.

Indeed, her young husband had no party, for he was the least suspicious man living in the world, and, except in matters of honour or war, he would make no plans and take no trouble.   Nor was Conachúr idle during his year of kingship.   His ability was marvellous, and his energy as wonderful.   Feuds that seemed to be endless were settled by him.   Foreign affairs that threatened or hung offered him no trouble.   But it was from the Judgement Seat that his fame spread most quickly.

13

"A fool," said the proverb, "can give
judgement, but who will give us justice?"
No question was so tangled but that swift
mind could pierce it; no matter was too
ponderous to be weighed by him, or too
light to escape his attention. He knew all,
he attended to all; everything he touched
was bettered, and men said that until that
year Ulster had never known prosperity, or
peace, or justice, but only the imitation of
these. Conachúr was every man's friend,
and in a short time every man was his.

Fergus returned to a court that had forgotten him, or that was so blinded by the
new prodigy that they saw nothing when
they looked elsewhere. It was held that
Fergus had actually resigned the kingship,
or that he had given it as a dowry to his
wife; and, although the young lord may
have been dismayed, the representation of
the nobles, and, in particular, the wit and
cajolery of his wife, arranged that matter,
so that he made no effort to regain his kingdom, and in a short time he was the
most devoted admirer of Conachúr in the
realm.

It is possible that Nessa left him then, or

that she died, but we do not hear of her
again.

Conachúr's married life may have been
happy, but it was short. At the end of
about eight months Clothru returned to
Connacht on a visit to the High King, her
father. We do not know what happened,
but a dispute arose between Clothru and her
youngest sister, Maeve.[1] Maeve struck a
blow that killed Clothru, and Conachúr's first
child was born in its mother's death agonies.

When this news came to Ulster Conachúr
set out to demand reparation or vengeance,
but when he beheld Maeve his ideas under-
went a horrible change. He had never seen
anything like this queenly creature. He
had not imagined that there could be in the
world a girl so wonderful as she, for she
was brave and able and of a marvellous
loveliness. Conachúr's hard mind would
not flinch when once his lusts were aroused.
His vengeance and his desire made common
cause. He married Maeve against her wish,
and without her consent, and he bore her

[1] It was this Maeve, anciently spelled "Madb," who
became afterwards "Mab" the Queen of the Fairies of
Spenser and Shakespeare.

15

back with him to Ulster, a queen, a captive, and, notwithstanding her crime, a deeply wronged woman.

Fergus mac Roy and Maeve, these were his victims, and from them there was to arise a story which would seem to the king as unending as time itself. Those two, and Deirdre!

CHAPTER III

DEIRDRE grew up in a place apart at Emania.
She saw no people of any kind, except Lavarcham, the king's "conversation - woman,"
and her women servants ; for always about
the castle where she lived there was a guard
of the oldest and ugliest swordsmen that
were in Ulster. Their duty was to let
nobody pass in or out of the castle grounds;
for it was the king's intention to outwit fate
as he had outwitted all else that had moved
in his path.

Thus she grew in gentleness and peace,
hearing no voice less sweet than the voice of
the birds that sang in the sunshine, or the
friendly calling of the wind she played with;
seeing nothing more uncomely than the
gracious outline of far hills, the many-
coloured sky that fled and was never gone,

the creatures that lived unmolested in the trees about the castle, and the wild deer that grew tame in nearby brakes. All that she knew was friendly to her and naught was rough. All that she drew nigh to stood for her approach. Naught fled from her, and she did not flee from anything.

Watching her, as she stood or sat or went, the wise Lavarcham used to lose her senses, for all that was beautiful was here gathered into one form, as in one true ray of the sun is all that is lovely of the sun. The running wind, and the wild creatures of the wood ; the folk from the Shí, the Bochanachs and Bananocks, and the aerial beings that are not seen, might have stayed to look at Deirdre, but had they stayed they could not have gone again, for they would have become eyes only, and they would have perished in beauty, gazing on it.

Lavarcham was a wise woman. She could not have occupied and continued to hold her position in Conachúr's household had she not been wise. She was known as the king's "conversation-woman," and she could indicate an unpleasant truth as delicately as a poet can express the dimple in a lady's chin.   But her real occupation, masked by the courteous word, was that of household spy.   She went to and fro in the vast palaces at Emania, and nothing passed there, whether among the nobles or the servants, that she was not privy to, or which the king was not thereafter acquainted with. She could adapt herself to any situation and to every society; and if her chatter with her kitchen-maids was jovial and in key, her conversation with a young princess or an old bard was not less balanced and elucidatory.

She had many things to teach a young girl, and she withheld no knowledge that could benefit the little one whom her heart had soon adopted as its own babe.   The virtues as well as the arts were part of her experience, so that Deirdre grew in the love of chastity, of industry, and of joyfulness.

In this way and in these teachings the years went by, unnoticed as years.   Day followed night, and night came after day in a timeless succession, each adding its unnoticeable little to her stature, its unseen tender curve to her limbs, its imperceptible deposit of memory to her mind.

But among the arts of which the tireless

Lavarcham spoke there was one she taught and retaught to Deirdre, and that art was Conachúr.

Although she had never seen the king yet the young girl knew him as a mother knows her baby. She could have recited his babyhood, his adolescence, and now his maturity. She knew, as only Lavarcham did, why he did such a certain thing, and by what progressions this stated consummation, marvelled at by others, had been arrived at. It was of infinite interest to Deirdre, but its inevitable effect was to stamp the unseen king with a seal of time, so that, although Lavarcham insisted he was only thirty-five years of age, the young girl's mind regarded him as one who could have been father and grandfather to a hill.

She reported to Conachúr at proper intervals as to her ward, and he, if he had wished, might have checked the passing years by his memory of the stories of Lavarcham told him of Deirdre learning to walk, and walking; of Deirdre learning to talk and talking: her teeth were counted to him as she cut them, and when she bruised her knee slipping down a bank, or when she wept for the cold fledgling she found on the path, or when she refused to weep in a thunderstorm, he was acquainted with the facts, and nodded at them gravely as they were told.

She had been a round thing, all surprise and fluff, like a young duck : she became a lank anatomy, all leg and hair and stare, like a young colt : then she became a wild thing, all spring and peep and run, like a young fawn ; and now she was what Lavarcham continued to report and dilate on.

But the king could not believe one half of the tale that Lavarcham told, for it seemed to him that such beauty as she reported was not credible, and he knew that women speak foolishly when they talk of beauty. He was, moreover, well satisfied with the queen who was with him then, Maeve, the lovely daughter of the High King.

CHAPTER IV

IT happened at last that Maeve came to the
decision which for a long time had been
forming in her mind. She decided that
she would not remain with the King of
Ulster any longer, and, having so decided
and faced all its implications, she was not
long in finding an opportunity to get away
from him. It is not right to say that she
"found" an opportunity, for she was of
those who create chance, and who do at all
times everything that is in their minds.

There were many reasons why she might
have been discontented as the wife of
Conachúr. The similiarity of their char-
acters, their equally imperious temperaments, their equally untiring and almost
identical habits of mind rendered each an
object of suspicion and endless cogitation

to the other. They could not rest together or apart, for each knew what, in certain circumstances, he or she would do, and unerringly credited the other with the performance of these surmised deeds. Thus leisure, which might have been profitably spent by either, was wasted by both in courteous ambuscades and counter or parallel schemes, so that the private habit of one was a perpetual cancelling of the private desires of the other, and a state of exasperation existed between them which, as it could not come to the surface and be faced or downfaced, ended by being a very poison to life.

In settling out these terms it is more proper to refer them to Maeve than to the king, for in the large conduct of his affairs he could escape from his household and forget in the Council Hall or the Judgement Seat that which his wife was given only the greater leisure to remember in her Sunny Chamber or among her servants and sycophants.

But matrimony had been poisoned for them at the very fountain, and a dear, detestable memory for Maeve was that her

husband had outraged her before he married
her, and that he had taken her then and
thereafter in her own despite.

If it had been a question of morality she
might have forgiven Conachúr almost before
forgiveness could be prayed for, but it was
not a moral violence she raged against. She
was a lady to whom nothing in the world
was so dear and instant as she was herself,
and that any man should lay an uninvited
hand upon her outraged her sense of pro-
priety as no general idea could have done.
But she was as courageous as she was
beautiful and as unblushing as either. The
world might have heard her statement of the
virtues she demanded in a husband, and if
the world was alarmed the young queen
permitted it to be as it pleased, on condition that it did not interfere with her, nor
question her wish.

"My husband," she said, "must be free
from cowardice, and free from avarice, and
free from jealousy; for I am brave in battles
and combats, and it would be a discredit to
my husband if I were braver than he.   I
am generous and a great giver of gifts, and
it would be a disgrace to my husband if he

were less generous than I am. And," she continued, "it would not suit me at all if he were jealous, for I have never denied myself the man I took a fancy to, and I never shall whatever husband I have now or may have hereafter."

It is possible that her husband did not fulfil these conditions as completely as Maeve desired. Of his courage there could be no doubt. He had proved that on many an opponent, and although there were better soldiers there were few who breasted danger with such gay violence. As to his generosity that might be questioned by one so whole-hearted as Maeve, for although he would give often and largely there might be more of calculation than of spontaneity in the gift: but it is in the third of her stipulations that Conachúr would probably be found wanting; for, given his temperament, his furious passions, his habit of command, and his endless cleverness, he should have been a very madman for jealousy. All clever men are jealous: it is one of the forms of egoism.

He must have tracked the discontented lady with the persistence of a bloodhound

and all the casual anonymity of a husband.
He would have been always just there in
the place where she least desired to see him;
and it is possible that gentlemen on whom
her eyes rested approvingly would disappear
before her eyes had adequately rested on
them. It may have seemed to Maeve that
some one like Conachúr was standing at
every corner in Emain Macha,[1] and that
at the few corners where he was not his
conversation-woman was, or some other
withered crone was there blaring hideously
on her yellow tusk and making a noise that
would annoy a young woman, but which
might absolutely terrify a young man.

She reviewed the situation and all the
subsidiary situations. She thought of what
her father, the High King, would say, and
knew how he should be answered and by
what arts he might be made an ally. She
thought of what her two sisters would urge,
but she thought of them negligently, considering that they would be more anxious to
avoid than to meet her. And she thought
of her third sister, about whom she need
speculate no more; and Maeve's hand that

[1] Emain Macha=pronounced Evan Maha.

26

struck the blow had been as steady as was her mind that contemplated its memory. Conachúr had come to demand vengeance and had exacted marriage. That was his vengeance, and she thought of the cold-minded, furious-blooded king in every alternation from astonishment to rage, and in every mood except that of fear, for she was not afraid of him, or of anything that lived.

CHAPTER V

HER immediate intention was to get away
from Ulster and so to order her conduct in
the meantime that the king, who suspected
everything and foresaw all, would have no
suspicion of this: therefore, if she cogitated
her plans she kept them in her own mind.
She would have no confidant until the action
was decided and the hour for it had struck.

And in this matter she had much to think
of. But she patiently resolved these com-
plexities, so that each went at last into its
place in her plan, and she had the leisure
to review and revise it until she could be
certain that nothing was forgotten and that
a perfect piece of machinery had been
created. The machine was not visible, but
it would appear as at a wave of her hand, and
it would begin to move at the hour of its

28

birth.   It was not by chance that this lady
was called by a masculine name,[1] for she had
patience and tenacity and a clear, cool head.

Had it been merely a question of getting
comfortably away there would have been
nothing in the prospect to exercise the queen.
She would have mounted her chariot, and,
whether her husband was looking or not
looking, she would have driven wherever she
wished to go: she would have driven over
him if he had stood in her way and through
his army if that had been unavoidable.   The
difficulty was that she did not intend to
leave with Conachúr the possessions she had
brought to Ulster and those that she had since
acquired, for the High King had endowed
his daughter in a manner befitting his condition and the rank she was to occupy; and, as
a wife's possessions were secured to her by the
law of the land, she did not intend to leave
Conachúr richer than he had a right to be.

It was the transport of this vast baggage
which exercised the queen.

She owned flocks of sheep, herds of cattle,
droves of horses and pigs.   These naturally
had multiplied during her residence at

[1] The word Maeve or Mab seems to mean "Intoxication."

Emain. She had vessels of gold and silver, of findriny and bronze. She had rings and bracelets; shoulder torques as big as plates, and breast brooches that were twice as big. She had pleasure chariots and war chariots; she had rich fabrics of linen embroidered with gold and silver thread; many-coloured, silken shawls with deep fringes of gold or with tassels and bobberies of silver. She had head-dresses of every material and metal. Bronze spears, each with an hundred loose rings of gold that clashed musically up and down the handle, and on each of the rings there chimed a little silver bell. She had shields and breastplates of solid silver and gold, and they were set out with patterns of dainty gems. There were quilts of silk and fur, cushions that delighted the head or the eye that rested on them. She had bird-cages of ivory and crystal. Beds that had been chipped out of monster blocks of amethyst. Cups of carved ivory, each with a different gem set inside at the bottom so that it twinkled at you while you drank. Chess-boards of precious metals, and each man on the board had occupied the cunning artificer a long year of his age to fashion it.

She had her own machinery for brewing and baking. What had she not got? Her dresses alone would pack a house and burst out through the roof and tumble down the glass of her Sunny Chamber like an untimely sunset for colour, and like a billow of the sea for exuberance.

She did not intend that as much as one thread of her threads should remain behind her in Emain Macha.

"No other queen shall waggle her toes in my draperies, nor enjoy what is proper for my enjoyment alone," thought Maeve.

Conachúr was preparing to go on a visit to Cairbre Niafar, King of Leinster, for he thought an alliance could be formed from which good might possibly come to Ulster. The neighbouring kingdom of Connacht had grown strong and stronger, and he knew that the people of that kingdom would be glad to think that Leinster and he remained at arm's length.

He would travel in state, and such a journey had to be organized carefully. Houses for rest and entertainment on the way must be arranged for. Heralds and messengers sent days in advance and dis-

positions made so that their reports might
be received on his journey. Several thousand men would be in his company, and
the shelter, feeding, and entertainment of
these had to be thought of. So for a little
time he was busy. But he was not too busy
to remark anything that might chance to be
remarkable.

Lavarcham sat with him in his retired
room at the centre of the Royal Branch.
From this room the great circular mass of
his palace radiated in all directions to its
ten-acre circumference, and in this deep-
placed, well-secured centre the king sat, as a
spider might sit in the middle of his gigantic
web. The room he occupied was sufficiently
large. The ceiling was an intricate medley
and very encrustation of carved wood, and
pushing out of that chaotic centre came a
great shoulder and a grotesque head which
held in its mouth a bronze chain with a
crystal ball swinging from it, and that ball
was so round and pure it seemed to be
one great drop of clear water. Sometimes
Cathfa came here, and would read matters
in the crystal to the king. The walls of

the room were panelled in polished red oak, and between each oaken panel was a panel of ruddy bronze, with a silver rail above it, and a golden bird was perched at the end of each rail ; so that the light from the torches gleamed gently again from the walls and multiplied itself in faint winks and reflections about the room.   There was one large chair there and a small stool.

Lavarcham was seated on the stool. She was permitted to rest in her master's presence, for she usually had much to say to him and he always found her interesting.

"Good my soul," said the king.   "I am glad that you are a woman."

"I am not badly contented about that myself," she smiled.

"For," he continued, "if you had been a man I should have been afraid of you."

"How so, master?"

"Because you could have taken my kingdom whenever you wanted it."

"Indeed, master, I would not accept a kingdom if I got one as a present.   There is too much responsibility and there is too much to do."

"It is no lie," he conceded.

33   D

"I like," she continued, "to do my work, and then I like to forget my work, but if I had the bad luck to be a king, or a queen, I should never again know what a rest meant, as you, my dear master, do not know what it is to rest yourself."

"Still," said the king smilingly, "the queen does get an occasional rest."

"A king wants rest but cannot get it, a queen, however, may not feel the need to rest, and may not wish for it."

"How do you intend that, my friend?"

"I mean that a woman gives herself up more than a man does, and when she so gives herself to love or power or hate, she gives all that she has, where a man may keep back something."

"But the queen, Lavarcham, as you have spoken of her, what do you think of her?"

"How would I dare to think about the queen, master?"

"Do you like her?" he insisted.

"She is very lovely."

"I perceive that you do not love the queen," said he, and then, after a moment, but severely—"do you love me, Lavarcham?"

34

"I do love you indeed," she answered gravely.

"But," he insisted, "do you love anybody else as well as me?"

"I love nobody else except my babe."

"Ah, that fabulous babe! Is she still getting new teeth, or what is it she is getting now?"

"She is getting to be a beautiful young girl, master."

"Ah, yes, you told me that."

"She is thirteen years of age."

"But tell me now, my heart, why did you draw the talk a moment ago to queens and their hate and restlessness?"

"Indeed, master, I did not draw the talk round in that way."

"Perhaps," he mused, "the queen has not treated you courteously."

"You are wrong indeed," she said happily, "for this whole week past the queen has been most kind to me."

"Ah!"

"And to-day she called me 'her Dear Branch, Lavarcham,' and spoke with me for an hour."

"Ah!" said Conachúr. "Have you been among her women?"

"I have, master."

"And her men?"

"They too."

"What have you found?"

"Nothing, master. Not a word, not a wink, not a stare, not a hesitation, not an eagerness, not a question. I found nothing."

"And in the queen what did you notice?"

"Affection for me, master."

"I wish I were not going away," said the king. He stood from his chair and strode weightily in the room.

"I too wish it," his companion agreed.

He halted and regarded her gravely.

"Be very friendly with the queen," he counselled.

But Lavarcham smiled pityingly at him.

"Why should I waste my time?" said she.

He nodded at that also, and became deeply and unhappily thoughtful.

CHAPTER VI

MAEVE had her own bodyguard of soldiers, close on one thousand men, who had come with her from Connacht, and from whom she refused to be parted. She was herself their captain, and each man of them was devoted to her. They were mostly her own countrymen, and she drilled and exercised and was good to them with untiring patience and skill. She was the mother of the force, but a wag called her the wife of the regiment. These thousand men were in Conachúr's mind as he arranged his visit to Leinster. He had often thought he must disband this force and replace it by his own men, or that he must win its allegiance and destroy it, so he also had been especially kind to the strange soldiers.

Now, on the eve of his journey, he thought

37

it would be a good thing to bring them
with him to Leinster; thus, as he explained
to Maeve, giving them entertainment and
exercise, while at the same time doing honour
to his queen and her native province. But
the proposition raised such a dreadful ire in
the queen, she trod the chamber in such
dudgeon and was so free in her speech that
Conachúr hastily and good-humouredly withdrew the suggestion; and bade her bear the
soldiers' discontent when they learned who
stood between them and one of the pleasantest
marches that a soldier could have.

Indeed, an argument with Maeve was not
to be lightly undertaken. It was likely to
last a long time in the first place, and in
the second, she had so precipitate a manner
of speech and so copious a command of
words that the listener's mind quickly began
to feel as if it were in a whirlpool, his head
would fly round and round, and he must run
away lest his brains burst out from his ears
and he die giddily.

No one but Conachúr could hearken to
Maeve's speech on such occasions, and he
only did it when he particularly wanted to.
For, at times, that which would drive

another man mad had a strangely soothing effect on him, and he could sit under that shrill tornado as peacefully as a daisy sits in the sunshine. At times, as one forces a restive horse much farther than it desires to go, he would impel into the brief tail-end of her sentence a philosophic and peace-ful interjection which acted on her as the spur on the horse, so that he would drive her beyond the very bounds of utterance, and she would at last, from sheer tongue-weariness, topple from the peaks of speech into a silence so profound that nothing it seemed could ever draw her thence again; and then Conachúr would talk to her sooth-ingly, reasonably, unforgivably, and it was Maeve would run.

But this time Conachúr fled: he was in no mood and had not the time for argu-ment; he knew she would not yield, and he was so angry and hurried that he could not be the patient, humorous, and watchful comrade he had intended to be.

When he spoke of this matter to Lavar-cham he did not speak with good humour, but he did not empty his mind even to the conversation-woman. It was not necessary.

39

"When I return from Leinster . . . !"
said he.

But the wise woman nodded only a half-
hearted agreement, for she thought that,
although it might only take two days to
bury a thousand men, it would take a long
time to bury those who would march to
avenge them.

The rage and agitation into which his
suggestion had thrown the queen was so
great that she fell ill, and could not accom-
pany her husband to Leinster. So that, as
on a previous occasion, he had to travel
without her, the understanding being that
she would take the road after him and,
travelling more lightly, could perhaps catch
on his company before they reached Naas,
the court and capital of the King of Leinster.

With his force, but unknown to it, there
went a youth—a long-striding, active, bull-
like young man with a freckled face and red
hair, and than whom there was no more
jovial person in all Ireland, for if a man was
striking at him with a spear he could make
that man laugh so much that he would not
be able to hit straight. His name was mac
Roth. He was Maeve's personal servant,

her herald. But just as the word "conversation-woman" cloaked another occupation for Lavarcham, so the word "herald" hid the same usefulness in mac Roth. He was Maeve's personal spy, but he also was her herald, and in after days, because of his knowledge, address, and courage, he was to be the chief herald of all Ireland.

He accompanied Conachúr's force, but he was not with it. He was a mile in advance, or a perch behind, or he was to the right of it just at a small distance, or he was looking from a hill on the left as the gay cavalcade and silver-shining chariots went by in the valley.

He accompanied them in that manner unseen for two days, and then, murmuring a blessing on them and on their encampment, he left them in the night, taking from them the loan of an unwatched horse, and he rode back by short cuts to Emain.

When he reached the palace he was able to report that the king had gone so far he could not easily turn back; and at that news Maeve's illness departed from her as suddenly as it had come.

In the morning she called for twenty of

the chief men of her bodyguard and gave
them careful, separate instruction. Then
she informed the domestics that her quarters
must be thoroughly cleaned while the king
was away, and that everything she owned
must be put out on the sunny lawn for
airing and counting.

The palace chamberlain came in great
haste, but that suave man was soothed by
Maeve and sent away with his dignity un-
hurt, but his mind exercised. He com-
municated his news to Lavarcham, who had
retired to the company of her "babe" outside Emania. Within the hour Lavarcham
despatched a flying messenger to Conachúr,
but just outside the city mac Roth, who was
waiting for him in a hedge, buzzed a spear
through that man's back as he went thundering past. But in the night Lavarcham, who
left little to chance, sent other messengers,
so that if some miscarried others would not.

But Maeve's plan was at work, the men
she had chosen for a particular part were
acting in that part, and inside of ten hours
her company was deployed behind her
baggage, her march to Connacht had begun,
and Conachúr was a bachelor again.

CHAPTER VII

IT was as well that the king was in Leinster at the time of Maeve's flight. Had he been nearer home he would have been obliged to do something, and, in such a situation, to do anything is to be ridiculous. He knew Maeve too well to imagine that she would return for a threat, yet he made the threats which seemed politic, for that was a matter of course.

But the messengers who bore these rigorous intimations to her father bore others to Maeve, and in these the son of Ness was humble as no one could imagine possible, and as his counsellors might not have deemed advisable.

There was no arrangement which she might have suggested that he would not have agreed to, but the difference between

43

them was too radical to be spanned by arrangements.

Maeve was proud; she was vain to boot, and could not consent to be second to any one. Living with Conachúr she had to be second, whatever he or she might desire. Indeed, living with him anywhere she would have to take second place, for the first place came to him so naturally, with such ease and finality, it could not be questioned or revoked, or contrived in any way.

More, and worse, she detested him for he had always dared her and succeeded. She, it is true, had dared him, and on this occasion had succeeded. But she could not live with him and dare him competently, which is just what he could do with her. Even if he abdicated the throne to her he would keep the sceptre, and she could no more take it from him than she could have abstracted the speed from the lightning. If she came back to Emania she would come back dead, or, should it happen that she did come back alive, the king would at last have to kill her or she would kill the king. Conachúr knew it, and at last renounced his vain embassies and hopes.

44

If we should wonder why he sent them, or why he should hope, the answer lay in his character.   That clever energetic man could not exist with a tame mate.   A mere bodily satisfaction he, sated in such satisfactions, would have exhausted in a week, and thereafter he would be without a refreshment which is as much of the mind as of the body, and which, to one of his temperament, has always most of the mind even when it seems fleshy to beastliness.   She satisfied cravings of his nature which he himself but dimly understood; and if, with her, the mistress was more apparent than the wife, therein lies the desire and doom of a clever man.

For he was diabolically clever, and, so, not wise, and, so, not great.   Only the great escape slavery, and he was the slave to his ego and would be whipped.   A great man would not, because he could not, take mean advantages.   But the manner in which Conachúr ousted Fergus from his throne will command the admiration of his peers only, and obtain from them the justification which success requires.   And yet he could retain the love of his victim, the trust of his people.   He was so near to greatness;

there were such sterling qualities running
with the egotism; he could be so mild in
difficulties, so clear-sighted in counsel; he
could be so staunch a friend; he could forgive with such royal liberality; he could
spend himself so endlessly for his realm.
Cúchulain did not think of him as a bad
man, nor did Fergus; and as to the latter,
he loved and honoured Conachúr above the
men of Ireland.   Was that a defect or a
merit in Fergus?   Was he too great or too
simple?   But it was not for clever tricks he
admired Conachúr, nor was it for tricks that
his people referred to him as the "wide-
eyed, majestic king."

However he bore the flight in public
he mourned for and craved for Maeve in
private, and the illness which comes to a
baulked will fell on him, corroding his mind
and his temper, so that even Lavarcham
left him as much alone as her duties permitted.

Again and again by an effort of the will
he would arouse from that sour brooding to
throw himself into work and into the grave
joviality which had once been his note; but,
as instantly, he would relapse visibly to any

46

eye, and might stare so sardonically and un-comprehendingly on a suppliant that the latter would be glad to go away with his tale unlistened to.

Matters were thus when a new plan began to brood in Lavarcham's mind, so that when she looked on her babe again it began to seem that she looked on a queen, for she intended to marry Deirdre to Conachúr.

All Ulster wished the king to marry again, for a celibate prince is a scandal to the people.

It was the constant effort of those responsible in the State to marry off a young prince almost as soon as he came to the age of puberty.   For such youngsters are great rovers, with appetites as gluttonous as dogs, and so care-free that they are surprised and indignant if others question the action which they do not themselves weigh.   It is certainly a hardship and a tyranny if a neighbour should constrain a neighbour's wife to his own domestic uses, but it is only a hardship because the affair occurs between equals, among whom friendly observances are due, and between whom equal respect is grounded.   Among equals anything that implies inequality is a punishable wrong: but there is no hardship when the superior takes what he carelessly desires. It is community of interests which makes equals, and the disturbance of this which makes enemies; but there is no community of interests between the prince and the subject, and no man is aggrieved by an action which can only affect his honour by increasing it. Nevertheless, so illogical is the mind of man, and so uncompromising is the sense of property, that men could be found who would interrupt with a spear the careless pleasure of a prince; and there were some, blacksmiths mostly and cobblers, who would take a cudgel to the king's majesty itself and beat it out of a warm bed.

So, when Lavarcham thought that she might conduct her ward between the lax arms of her sovereign, she but harboured an idea which every male person in the realm who had a wife, a sister, or a daughter, hoped for with fervour.

Nor did the idea occur only to her.

Within a month of Maeve's disappearance more young ladies began to appear in Emania than had been noticed there previously, so that Conachúr, had he been in a condition to observe such things, might have noticed that Ulster had begun to blossom like the rose.

But plottings such as these were of small use in the case of a man like Conachúr, and it is likely that the first person to know what should be done and what was expected from the head of the State was the king himself. His duty as a king would point him the way: the necessity to repair what had been damaged would claim his mind; and the desire to forget by replacing would be even more insistent; for if a hair of the dog that bit you is the specific against drunkenness, it is a medicine against love also, and is, alas, the only one we know of.

Therefore the king did for a while take a fevered interest in the ladies of his court, but he found, so jaundiced was his eye, that they were neither worth looking at nor worth talking to, and he did not grudge their companionship to any man.

To Lavarcham, at last, he opened his mind.

"I must marry, Lavarcham, my soul."

"There is plenty of time for that, master," said the wily woman.

"While I have no wife," Conachúr replied, "the people will talk of the wife I had, and the only way to stop that is to give them something else to talk of."

"It is true, indeed," said Lavarcham.

"I foresee," he continued, "that I shall be compelled to marry some one I do not care for."

"In that case, master, you will be saved the trouble of choosing, for you may take the first that comes."

"They seem to resemble one another like peas in a pod. Are women all alike, my friend?"

"They are much of a pattern, master."

"And yet——," said the king, brooding deeply on one that had fled.

"Our little ward," Lavarcham continued thoughtfully, "is rather unusual."

"What age is she now?" said the dull king.

"Sixteen years and a few months."

"So much. We must think of marrying her to some friend. Perhaps one of our

kinsmen of Scotland.   I must be reminded
again of it."

"Come and see her, master, and then
you will be able to decide how she should
be disposed of."

"I shall go to see her some day."

CHAPTER VIII

DEIRDRE'S education in the art of the king
continued, but it proceeded now somewhat
obliquely to its former trend.

What woman in Lavarcham's place could
avoid treating her master's later affairs without something of sentimentality creeping
into the terms? And what young girl
could regard Maeve otherwise than as a
heroine for having dared so shocking a
scandal, and such a round of perils. As
Lavarcham detailed Maeve, Deirdre inter-
preted her, and at the close of the statement
the judgement of each was so different, so
opposed, that a third person might have
marvelled at the tricks the understanding
can play; for what was black to the one
was not only white to the other, but it was
crimson and purple and gold; and what

was treachery to Lavarcham gleamed on Deirdre like a candid sunrise.

We assimilate knowledge less through our intellects than through our temperaments; and a young person can by no effort look through the eyes of an older. There are other ways by which a mutual perception can be so deflected that the same thing is not similarly viewed, and so Lavarcham's appreciation of Maeve's conduct would differ from Conachúr's, as his would be unlike Cathfa's or Bricriu's or Fergus mac Roy's, and as these would be obscure to one another. The element of self-interest in each would act as a prism, and each would understand as much of the tale as he desired to understand, but no more, and would forgive or condemn on these arrested findings.

To Lavarcham Maeve's flight was treachery and deserved punishment; but it was not, in her thought, a misfortune for which even Conachúr need weep. She had thoroughly disliked Maeve, for though she could impose on every one she could not impress that imperious lady, and she had never dared tell one half of Maeve's doings

lest the violent queen should suspect, and
loose a slash that would cut her in two
halves in the very presence of the king.

The departure of Maeve meant also the
departure of mac Roth, and to be free from
that jovial, crafty eye was so great a relief
that Lavarcham could have wept in thank-
fulness ; for to be a spy is a simple thing,
an occupation like any other, but to be spied
upon when one is a spy is a monstrous inver-
sion of what is proper, and might easily give
one palpitations of the heart.

Mac Roth had her frightened, and could
have cowed her any time he wished. In
her own craft he was her master, for, after
all, she was only a household spy, but he was
a—spy. She could glean from the kitchen
or the Sunny Chamber everything that was
there ; but she must have walls about her and
work behind those ; while mac Roth did not
mind whether he was in a room or in a forest ;
he would spy in a bee-hive ; he would spy
on the horned end of the moon ; he would
spy in the middle of the sea, and would know
which wave it was that drowned him, and
which was the wave that urged it on.

Lavarcham was not only glad that Maeve

was gone, she was jubilant; and, moreover, it gave her an opportunity that she could scarcely have hoped for to advance her babe in life without parting from her, and to strengthen all her own grips on fortune.

Hitherto, when she had spoken of Conachúr to Deirdre she spoke of the king's majesty, but now, insensibly, she began to talk of a great man bowed under misfortune and a proper subject for female pity. But she could not wipe out the king's majesty with that sponge nor alter one lineament of the portrait she had taken ten years to limn.

The king persisted for Deirdre, stern and aloof and almost incredibly ancient, looming out from and overshadowing her infancy like a fairy tale; and was he not contemporary with Lavarcham, herself old enough to be remembered but not thought of. Deirdre was interested in the king as she was interested in the people of the Shí,[1] without expectation, and with a little fear.

But to her reasonings and objections Lavarcham had one answer:

"My soul and dear treasure, you cannot speak about men for you have not seen any."

[1] The Shí=Fairyland.

55

And at last one day Deirdre replied:

"Indeed, mother, I have seen them, these men you tell me of."

Lavarcham stared at her.

"And," the gleeful child continued, "I have spoken to them."

Her foster-mother became smoother than silk, and soft as the lap of kindness.

"Tell me about that, my one love, and tell me how men seem to you now that you have seen them."

"It is not hard to tell," replied Deirdre; "men are as ugly as donkeys, and," she continued, "they are just as nice."

"As ugly and as nice as donkeys!" Lavarcham quoted in a daze.

"Yes, mother, and I love them because they are so nice and ugly and good."

"But what men are you talking of, my star?"

"I am talking of the men outside the walls."

"The guards?"

"Of course."

"And when did you see them?"

Deirdre laughed.

"Why, I have seen them ever since I

was that height," and she poised her hand two feet above the ground.

Lavarcham laughed at her and waggled a reproving finger.

"You have not seen them very often, all the same."

"I have indeed," the girl replied triumphantly. "I have seen them every day of my life for the last ten years."

"And you spoke to them?"

"Of course I did. I know every one of them as well as I know you."

"You do not, Deirdre!"

"I do so: I know their names, and who they are married to, and how many children they have. O, I know everything about them."

"Sly little fairy of the hills," cried her perplexed guardian, "you are poking fun at Lavarcham."

"I surely am not," Deirdre replied positively.

"Well, tell me about these men that are ugly and nice like donkeys."

"Very well," cried Deirdre, "I shall prove to you that I know them."

"You must know," she narrated, "that

each of these men is always at the same
place outside the wall, but some of them
are on guard during the day-time and others
are on guard during the night. Every
second week they change this order and the
ones that have been on duty in the night
take up day duty, and the day men replace
them; and so they change and change
about, year in and year out, under the
charge of two captains and eight ancients.
There are an hundred of these men alto-
gether; twenty-five of them march from
point to point all around the walls during
the day, but in the night seventy-five men
march to and from smaller points. In the
day also, one captain and two ancients
march around and overlook the twenty-five
guards, but a captain and six ancients march
about the men who are on duty at night."

"Ah-ha," cried Lavarcham, "you have
been told all this by the women servants."

"They only tell me tales of the men of
Dana and of the Shí, and of how their
children were born, and of the proper way
to cure pimples."

"Well, tell me more," sighed Lavarcham,
"until I see what it is that you do know."

58

"The captain of the troop is named Daol, but the men call him Fat-face. He has fourteen children and is unhappily married, for he has told me many times that if he had a better wife he would be a better man. One day when his wife was baking him a cake she baked a spell into it, so that, although he had never felt ache or pain before, he was racked all that day with torments ; and ever since, when the moon changes and the wind goes round, he gets pains in his bones, and he beats his wife when he gets home on the head of it."

"You are certainly acquainted with this Fat-face."

"I love him. He wears a great leathern belt with a sword hung from it, and, when he orders the men, he thrusts his two hands down through the belt, stretches his legs very wide apart, and roars at them—but how he roars! 'Troop!' he roars : 'turn by the right hand : trot'; and all the dear old men trot with their heads down very thoughtfully, until he roars at them to stop trotting, and then they all sneeze, and talk about their feet.

"Sometimes he lets me drill the men."

"He should not," said Lavarcham.

"He had to," the girl replied, "for I threw stones at him from the top of the wall until he agreed to let me do it. But that was a long time ago."

"He should have reported all this."

"Do you mean he should have told on me?" cried Deirdre indignantly. "Indeed I should like to see Fat-face daring to tell anything about me. Why, the men would beat him if he told. I would get down off the wall and beat him myself."

CHAPTER IX

THIS conversation greatly exercised Lavarcham, and she cast about for some means whereby she might restrain her ward. It was waste of time, as she quickly saw, for who that has been charged with a young person aged sixteen has not been forced at last to renounce all real guardianship.

At that age the time has passed for prohibitions, and the time has not yet come when advice can be listened to except in the form of flattery. The young body is eager for experience, and will be satisfied with nothing less actual, so the older person must grant freedom of movement or be run to death by that untiring energy. For a while the youngster will drink deeply, secretly, of her own will, and will then disengage for herself that which is serious and enduring

61

from that which is merely pleasant and unprofitable. For all people who are not mentally lacking are sober-minded by instinct, and when the eager limbs have had their way the being looks inwardly, pining to exercise the mind and to equip itself for true existence.

At fourteen years of age Deirdre was not the untameable little savage she had been at twelve, and at the age of sixteen she had begun to long for some one to whom she might submit her will and from whom she could receive the guidance and wisdom and refreshment which she divined to be in herself, but which she could not reach.

Her fury of activity would be broken by equal periods of languor, wherein she would sit as in a daze, staring at the sky and not seeing it, or looking at the grass with a vague wonder as to what this was upon which her eyes were resting. Wild creatures or tame would trot or amble before her, but she was only conscious of a movement without a form. A bird might light and flirt and hop and fly, and her forsaken mind would touch those facts without gaining information from them, and would lose itself behind the movement vaguely, blindly, dizzily, until the bird mixed into the sky and the sky rounded and receded and disappeared, leaving her eyes nothing to rest on and her errant mind without any support.

She would look on her arms, as they hung helplessly in the grass, and wonder that they were so unoccupied, and wonder that they were so empty. And an oppression came to her heart, gentle enough, but without end, as though something stirred there that could not stir, as though something sought to weep and could not weep; so that she must weep for it, and grieve for it, and be of a tenderness to that unknown beyond all the tenderness that she had sensed about her. And these idle tears would arouse, or assuage her, so that she wondered why she wept, and she would leap from such nonsense and speed away like one distraught with excess of life and energy.

She would become affectionate then. She mothered the cow and its lanky calf; the peeping rabbit and her popping brood. The shaggy mare and her dear, shy foaleen, an arm about each neck, listened to a conversation they loved and seemed to understand. When she tried to leave them they trotted behind with gentle, persistent feet and eyes of such pleading that she must run passionately back, crying that she would come again, that she would surely come back to them on the morrow. There was not a nest she did not know of, and the young grey mother, snuggling among the leaves, would look gravely out at the grey eye that peeped within, and would hearken to a cooing so delicious, so burthened with love, that her broody hour would pass uncounted, and she would forget her mate abroad, and the wide airs of the tree-tops.

At night the moon could woo her so passionately she must forsake her bed and go tiptoe among dark corridors until she came into the presence. What wild counsel did she receive from the glowing queen! Or was it the unmoving quietude that whispered without words; intimations of—what? Shy touches at the heart, so that she, who feared nothing, would look about her, startled as a young roe, who senses something on the wind, and flies without more query.

How lovely to her was that suspense and fear, when her every nerve thrilled to a life more poignant than she had surmised; when something that did not happen was perpetually occurring; when, as it were in a moment, she might be told—what secrets! or be cautioned of something imminent and advised!

She lost herself in the moon, wooing it, wooed by it, until she seemed to move in the moon, and the moon to move in her; a sole whiteness, a sole chillness, one equal potency—For what? for that, for it, for something, for nothing, for everything. She submitted her destiny to the delicate sweet lady of the sky, and one night, beckoned to, drawn at, surrounded, a small moon shining in the moon, she went on and on, passing the grass to the turf; leaving the turf for the stony places; from there to the wall, and over the wall also; so lightly, so imperceptibly, so moonily, the drowsy guard did not see; or if he saw 'twas but a moonbeam that rose and fell, that fluttered and faded, that lapsed over a piece of hollow ground and glimmered away on the slope, merging in the silver flood and the shades

of ebony, and gone while he rubbed his
eyes.

So she marched towards destiny.

She went among the darkness of trees,
and farther, where the wood grew thin,
into a dappled dancing of jet and silver;
and, beyond, to where young voices called
and called and called.

Such fresh young voices she had never
heard before, used as she was to the dry,
clipped utterance of Lavarcham, the tooth-
less mumble of the servants, the rusty bawling
of Fat-face as of an obstinate door that told
of aches and reluctances, and the wheezing
and grunting of his stiff companions.   She
stayed listening to those voices, young as
her own, and as sweet; rattling like the
waters that tumble and ride in the river;
chattering like a nestful of young birds in
spring; soaring up and falling down with
an infinite eagerness and joy; until it
seemed that a lark's song and the flight of a
swallow had come together and fused into
one streaming of sound.

Standing behind a vast black tree her
astonished heart released itself in tears, and
she wept for her cloistered youth, and

66

for all that she did not know she had missed.

Then boldly she trod forward and sat herself resolutely at the camp-fire of the sons of Uisneac.

CHAPTER X

THEY received her with the scant show of surprise which youth, so proud of appearances, so jealous of its own dignity, extends to the unknown, and, after the brief word of welcome, and swift surmising glance, the conversation which she had interrupted renewed itself, perhaps a shade more boisterously because they had been surprised, a little more hardily because they knew one was listening who was not of their company and might be critical.

Soon, in their own despite, something ceremonious crept on them, overpowering their boisterousness and making each self-conscious, until, by the inevitable degrees, silence hovered and threatened about the fire, and for moments nothing moved but the eye that flickered and wandered into woodland vistas, where delicate dark trees stood rimmed in silver, and everything on the ground crept and fled as the boughs swayed and the moon spilled through them.

But the silence only endured long enough for the look to become frank and the mutual examination a judgement. Then the eldest of the three boys seized the conversation to himself and upheld it, for he saw that their guest was so afflicted with shyness that she could not move hand or foot, and could not have replied if one had addressed her.

He spoke for occupation also, because, having looked at her, he feared or was too shy to look again; feared, too, that the others might observe his embarrassment; and, being one to whom action was a first habit, he did what he could do when he found that there was something which he could not do.

He did it well.

Listening to him Deirdre knew what was the mid surge of the stream she had listened to, the top singing of the song she had heard. This was the lark sustained at the top of flight, and the others the mazy pattern of the swallows' wings. Listening she could collect herself; and, in a while, daring to

hear, she dared to see, and then she heard
no more; for when the eye is filled the ear
is no more attended, and all that may be of
beauty is there englobed, radiant, sufficient,
excessive.

How should I paint Naoise[1] as Deirdre
saw him, or show Deirdre as she appeared
to the son of Uisneac? For than Deirdre
there was no girl so beautiful unless it might
be Emer the daughter of Forgall, soon to
be wooed by Cúchulinn; and Naoise himself could not be bettered by any among
the men of his land unless it was by the
"small, dark man, comeliest of the men of
Eirè," Cúchulinn himself.

When we endeavour to tell of these
things words cannot stand the trial. It may
be done by music, or by allusion, as the
poets have always done, saying that this girl
is like the moon, or like the Sky-Woman of
the Dawn, when they would indicate a beauty
beyond what we know; and that she is like
a rose when they would tell of a gentle and
proud sweetness; that her wrist is crisp and
delicate like the delicate foam that mantles
on a sunny tide; that the wise bee nestled

[1] Naoise=pron. neesh-eh.

in her bosom, finding more of delight there than the hive gives; that she walks as a cloud, or as a queen-woman of the sky, seen only in vision, so that all other sights are but half seen thereafter and are scarcely remembered.

In these grave ways we may approach perfection, indicating distantly that which cannot be unveiled in speech; or we may tell of the abasement which comes on the heart when beauty is seen; the sadness which is sharper than every other sadness; the despair that overshadows us when the abashed will concedes that though it would overbear everything it cannot master this, and that here we renounce all claim; for beauty is beyond the beast, and like all else of quality it can only be apprehended by its equal and enjoyed where it gives itself.

Still, they were young, and with young people impressions that come quickly go as fast. They have so much in common; their interest in the present is so quick; their faith in the future so fearless; their memory of tenderness is so recent, and their experience of treachery so small, that friendship comes easier to them than enmity does, and trust grows where suspicion withers; so in a little time they were again at ease, and when the food they had been preparing was eaten they knew one another and were friends.

Naoise was then almost nineteen years of age, his brother Ainnle, seventeen, and Ardan more than fourteen, while Deirdre herself was almost a full sixteen years.

If she had listened before as it were to the chattering of a brook or the outburst of a flight of birds, she now listened to a talk that was like a mill-race for exuberance, and the cawing of a colony of rooks for abundance; and yet, when she remembered it afterwards, she could not remember much, or she recollected that they laughed more than they spoke. For the talk consisted more of questions than anything else, and the answer to each query was in nearly all cases an outbreak of laughter and another question.

Do you remember the day Cúchulinn came playing hurley into Emain?

And the way he took the troop under his protection?

72

And the night he went out a boy and came back a hound?

Jokes, hinted at, that had been played on foster-fathers; grisly jokes of the first combat of a comrade who had left his head where his feet should be; questions that hinted at outrageous parties in the night, when the boys chased a wild boar and their fathers and foster-fathers hunted them; of punishments that had been evaded as a fox dodges a dog, and behold, when safety had been found, there was the punishment awaiting them.

They were young, but they had killed; and they rocked with glee as they told by what marvellous strategy they had got in the lucky blow, and how the champion had gone down never to rise again, and they had trotted home squealing and squawking with joy, with a head surveying the world from the top of a spear, and it grinning down on them as joyously as they chattered up at it.

Names that Deirdre was unfamiliar with, and some that she knew from the servants' talk, flew from mouth to mouth. Conall the Victorious, Bricric the Prank-player,

Laerí called the Triumphant, Fergus mac
Roy, these youngsters spoke of as familiarly
as she might have told of the birds in her
garden, and criticized them with all the
unsparing freedom of youth.

They did not consider that these great
men were in any way superior to themselves:
the contrary was certainly in their minds.
It was evident that Ardan and Ainnle thought
their brother Naoise could whip any other
champion rather easily: but Naoise was
modest and would say nothing for or against
this theory.

Deirdre was as convinced as the boys were
that Naoise could beat any combination of
champions that might have the ill-luck to
move against him. She knew it from his
complexion, from his curling hair. Oh!
she knew it from a variety of proofs, and
she was inclined to be angry when he argued
with the younger boys that Cúchulinn[1]
was the greatest man alive. But on that
subject the agreement was so unanimous, so
hearty, that she might doubt but could not
question it.

"What I should like," said Ainnle,

[1] Cúchulinn = pron. Ku-hullin.

"would be to see a fight and a combat between our Cúchulinn and Fergus mac Roy."

"That would be a fight indeed," said Naoise, "but we shall never see it.   They love each other."

"It would be a queer thing," said Ainnle, "if a boy were to fight with his own foster-father."

"I heard that a boy once did, and killed him too," said Ardan.

"Who did?   Who did?"

"I forget his name."

"Because you never heard it."

"Our young Ardan makes things up in his head," said Naoise, in a fatherly voice, while Ardan hid his blushes by attending to the fire.

"Do you think," Ainnle inquired, "that Cúchulinn could beat Fergus if they fought?"

Naoise regarded that query judicially.

"I don't know indeed," he replied.

"I think Cúchulinn could beat anybody," Ardan broke in.

Naoise continued, without regard to his youngest brother:

"It was Fergus that taught Cúchulinn

75

all his battle feats, and Fergus knows everything that the Cú knows, but it may easily
be that our Cúcuc does not know all the
things that Fergus knows."

"Fergus," cried Ainnle indignantly,
"would not keep a thing back, for he wants
Cúchulinn to be the best champion in Eirè."

"I think that is true," replied the very
judicial Naoise, "but there are some things
a fighter knows and can't teach even if
he wants to. They are not tricks, they are
what Conachúr calls ways, and Fergus has
'ways' in combat, as if he had been born
in a fight and could go to sleep in it if he
wanted to."

"Do you remember," cried Ainnle, "the
champion that stopped to scratch himself
while he was fighting?"

"Ho, ho," laughed Ardan.

"And the other champion chipped his
hind end off while he was bending," gurgled
Ainnle.

"Wasn't that man a great fool?" said
Ardan solemnly.

"No," laughed Naoise, "it was just that
he thought he had time to do it. I saw
that combat. It must have been that a

wasp or hornet slid into his leg band. He gave a jump and a quick bend to get at his leg, but the other man jumped after him; then he gave another great jump and another bend, and he got a little trip at the same time—that is how the other champion slashed him; but everybody was laughing so much that his life was spared, so he kept his head if he lost his tail."

"Ho, ho, ho!" roared Ardan.

And it was his laughter that made Deirdre part with a squeal of glee which so astonished her that she leaped to her feet and fled among the trees, and so home.

She had not spoken to the boys beyond the word of blessing and greeting which could not be omitted. Ardan and Ainnle considered that it was quite right a girl should be silent in the presence of champions, but Naoise thought it was a pity she did not speak, for he was inclined to fancy that her voice would be pleasant to listen to.

CHAPTER XI

IF it rested only with the boys the girls might go unmarried, for boys have urgent interests and have little of the leisure for dream which girls enjoy.

They feel, moreover, at a loss in that art wherein a girl seems instinctively wise; for as a young bee will undertake untaught the curious angles and subtle perfections of his home so a girl will adventure herself in love without misgiving and without teaching.

The secret of the bee and of the girl is that they give their whole minds to their idea; and this powerful concentration, wherein the being comes to a oneness of desire, moves to its ends as unerringly as a bird wings to the sole hedge he aims for among all the hedges of a country-side.

So, although Naoise did think again of their visitor, his thought of her was but one

among many, for he had grave businesses in
hand, and, except when he slept, his leisure
for dreaming was limited.

He had long since left the Boy Troop at
Emania. He had performed the feats by
which an apprentice rises to be a master,
and a full two years had passed since
Conachúr, in the presence of a solemn con-
course, had received him into the Red
Branch, and bestowed on him the armour
which he had won, and the shield which he
would honourably guard.

He was a gentleman by birth, but he was
now a soldier also, and must lift his hand for
those who besought protection or against
those who derided it. He would move
habitually where death urged about him at
no greater distance than the length of a
spear, and he would look upon death as being
so instant a part of life, that he must woo
the one as earnestly as he loved the other.

His thought of Deirdre was also com-
plicated by the knowledge that she was his
master's ward, and his personal loyalty to
Conachúr was such that he would not dwell
even in imagination on that which belonged
to the king.

Stories of Deirdre had long ago come abroad. The fact of her lonely keeping lent a romantic charm to gossip, and all that was said about her was stressed by the singular condition of her birth and upbringing. The old servants hinted and blinked and nodded, indicating thus a beauty for which there was no parallel; and the ancient guards, partly in brag, partly in truth, lent an aid to the spread of the Deirdre rumour.

These things, however, were to be talked about, but they were not to be further looked into, for she belonged to the king, and curiosity itself went lightly in the presence of that notable fact. Therefore, so far as a young man could, Naoise put Deirdre out of his mind, or only remembered her as a delicious apparition, and he warned his brothers that they must on no account mention her escapade.

But if this was the case with the boy it was not so with the girl. For good or ill her imagination had been captured, and through it her senses had awakened. Her fancies had now a home to fly to, and while the unrest proper to her years grew as stealthily as her limbs it was no longer un-noted. She had a direction and she leaned there as ardently and unconsciously as a flower turns to the sun.

Now she became a creature of another reverie; no longer staring vaguely into space but looking there, and seeing what even the wise Lavarcham could not surmise.

This powerful brooding of desire is a magical act, and the object of it does not remain entirely unaffected; for even if no coherent message is despatched the unrest is shared in however diffused a form, and it may be that in sleep Naoise was no longer the master of his dreams.

But the real scope of an action is with the actor, and Deirdre, brooding on Naoise, was Deirdre brooding on herself, and taking conscious control and direction of her own growth and culture. Lavarcham noticed the difference; for when she spoke to the girl she was replied to by the woman, and she sensed in her ward something intract-able, obedient still, and yet as removed from her cognizance and so from her control as she was herself from the cognizance of any person about her.

CHAPTER XII

THEREFORE, when she next spoke to the king her mind was stirred by uneasiness, and she had all that feeling of haste and work to be done which comes to us when we seem void of direction and are yet spurred on to an intuitive urgency.

"Lavarcham, my soul," said Conachúr, "you always get your way, for you insist and insist, and at last whatever you wish must be done or there is no peace in the household or the kingdom."

"In good truth," said Lavarcham, "I do not recognize my fault this time."

"We forget by repetition," cried the king, "and you have so dinned our ears these ages past about your babe that I must consent to see her or perish from your importunities."

"That I am glad of," replied Lavarcham, "for she is growing and needs other guidance than I can give. You should find her a husband," said the crafty woman.

"That must be done," the king murmured.

He was silent for a few minutes, for the thought of marriage reminded him of his own adventures in that condition, and when he spoke it was with an elaborate carelessness?"

"Have you heard any news of the High King?"

"I have heard, but it is only a rumour, that his daughter, the queen Maeve, has been married again, and that the High King has bestowed on her the kingdom of Connacht."

"A number of our young men," said he, with a hard smile, "have for long enough disliked that kingdom and its people: it may become difficult to keep them from crossing the border."

"One of their men," said Lavarcham, "crosses the Black Pig's Dyke often enough."

"And, woe on it," said Conachúr with

83

a cheerful laugh, "he gets back again. We must strengthen the Connacht marches, or that man will make our fortifications the laughter of all Ireland. It is Cet mac Magach you speak of."

"Conall Cearnach's uncle indeed," Lavarcham replied.

"But Conall crosses their borders too," said the king. "My memory is weakening," he continued, "what is it that Conall boasts of?"

"He boasts that he never goes to sleep without the head of another Connachtman lying in the crook of his knees."

"Some day he may forget to remember that Cet mac Magach is his uncle, and if he brings that head home we shall give it an honourable welcome. But about your babe, I shall go and look at her to-morrow. All your over-statements will crowd on your mind to-morrow, my poor friend, and you will be very unhappy."

"Indeed," Lavarcham admitted, "we look with a loving eye on the person we love and so may see less or more than is visible to other people."

"In love," Conachúr replied, "we see

84

only what we love to see, and as that is un-
real we should not look lovingly on anything, and so we may get sight of what is
really visible."

"It is true, master," said Lavarcham
humbly.

"It is with such an eye that I shall look
on your babe to-morrow."

"Alas! my poor Deirdre," said Lavarcham.

"The Troubler has not given much
trouble yet," laughed Conachúr.

CHAPTER XIII

LAVARCHAM went home.

The sense of urgency and unmeditated haste which for some time had been in her mind was greater than ever, as though she were being pressed to an action, thoroughly comprehended indeed, but for which she had no plan and no explanation. There was something to be done: she knew what it was but could not state it: and there was also something which prevented its accomplishment; and she was similarly aware and unaware of what this latter obstruction was.

This sense of being controlled without being consulted, of being given a key without being told what door it opens, is common to all people who plan and are not sufficiently disengaged to observe that they are being overridden by their own contrivance; for

there is a point up to which we control
desire, but at the stage where other peoples'
interests intersect ours those alien desires
and our own meet: they cease to be many
and become one thing, and we are ridden
in community by the jinn we liberated.　But
we know with a profound, unconscious
certitude all that is happening, and are
enlisted for those intuitive purposes beyond
the control of interest or prudence or reason.
Habit alone remains to guide us in these
trackless ways, and it was her habit of
verbal reticence which calmed Lavarcham.

Her first impulse had been to tell Deirdre
with a rush that the king was coming to
see her on the next day.　Her second impulse was cautious.　If I tell this, she
thought, the child will not sleep all night,
and she will be heavy-eyed and dull before
the king.

Therefore she did not mention the matter
to Deirdre.

But she was no longer the calm lady
whom the world knew.　She would sit
down and stand up, and go wandering from
room to room, and return from these ram-
blings, to begin them all over again.　She

87

sat by Deirdre's side and took her hand, peering long and earnestly into the face she loved: dwelling on the set of her eyes, the line of her cheek, the poise of her lips and her chin: watching how her teeth shone and disappeared as she spoke, what her tongue looked like as it became visible for a short red flash: looking now at her ears and now at her hair; or standing well away to take her in as a girl, as a completion, with all details merged and the human unit standing full formed at the eye.

She cogitated what dress Deirdre should wear on the morrow: what ornaments for her neck and hair; and then she thought, in a fever of inspiration, that she would take no thought of these: that the girl should be dressed even more plainly than usual: that there should be no ornaments upon her of any kind: that there should be nothing to look at but the girl herself with her hair for a crown, and her eyes for all other attraction: the light eagerness of her limbs should be their own witness: the colour of her cheeks should be sufficient wonder for any eye.

And again she thought that men do not

understand these things at a glance; that
they are used to looking for that which they
have already seen; and that they spend time,
not so much in appreciating that which is
present, as in trying to account for the
absence of that which they had expected to
see.   And she remembered again that it
was Conachúr himself who was coming, with
a mind which would ponder exactly what
was presented to it, and an eye that would
regard no more than could be seen.

She determined, in terror, that she would
not prepare Deirdre in any way for the visit,
and that until she was called into the presence
the child should know nothing even of an
impending visitor.

She arranged that this should happen,
and at the accustomed hour the torches
were quenched and the folk of the household betook themselves to their beds.

CHAPTER XIV

BUT at the hour she considered suitable Deirdre rose again from her bed.

She could not rest there, although she lay with the endless patience of a cat, staring hour after hour into the gloom and seeing in it more of radiance than the sun could show.

She was living at last.

The sense that all the morrows were provided for, and that all the minutes of all the morrows were calculated and ordained, dropped from her for ever, for she had become at last an identity instead of a puppet to be pulled here and ordered there, and to do only what was willed by other people; for first the imagination awakes and then the senses and lastly the will, when the urge of life is focussed.

Thinking of these other people, of Lavarcham and the grisly servants, of the ramshackle, sneezing guards, all ringing her about from freedom, a sense of rage came into her soul, so that at moments she was no longer a girl but a wild cat, and she could have scratched and screeched and died in one senseless outrage.

Her mind, too, was overflowing with that same sense of urgency, as though something clamoured to be done immediately and at a pace faster than limbs could manage. What was it she wanted? She did not know, but she knew definitely that she wanted it with a whole uncontrollable mental greed that made of her a person she did not recognize and could not battle with.

But with all that tumult of mind she was patient with the marvellous patience of youth, for no grown person has one tithe of the patience of a child, who, from the hour he is born until the day when he snatches liberty from reluctant elders, leads a life that is one unending lesson in attending. They can wait, for they know that the future is theirs and will come to them over whatever obstruction. And she could wait.

When Lavarcham trod softly in her chamber she pretended to be asleep, and amused herself staring behind closed lids at the red light which the torch carried even through that darkness. She thought her guardian would never go away, and lifting one scrap of an eyelash she saw Lavarcham brooding upon her with such a fixity of attention, with so profound a scrutiny, as surprised her. So curious and prolonged was this examination that she almost opened her eyes to demand a reason for this scrutiny from the face of ivory and jet that was bending over hers. But she did not do so, for young people can bear starings and examinations which would madden them later in life, and are able to consider that affairs which actually circle upon them are yet not their business.

Lavarcham sighed deeply, and as in a passion of what?—fear, hope, doubt—and then the light began to recede, and went farther away, and disappeared.

Deirdre knew every motion that Lavarcham made at night. Now she did this, next she would do that, afterwards she would do such another thing: an unvarying sequence of small details which she had watched or listened to since the first hour that she was able to watch or listen.   So that when she came from her bed she left it with the certainty that she might do so, and that all the habitual details had culminated in the habitual sleep into which Lavarcham placed herself even when it did not overcome her.

CHAPTER XV

THE moon was at her last quarter, a pale thin sickle that shone and disappeared and reappeared in a mass of hastily scudding cloud. During that eclipse obscurity fell on the air, and a yet vaster quietude enveloped the earth. Then the sickle reappeared, and with it more than the darkness lifted. Something even more mysterious than darkness vanished intermittently; that brooding as of an infinite presence seemed to recede, and the normal world, beautiful and comprehended, came silverly to the view.

Through these glooms and visions Deirdre fled, observing every shadow as a hare does, who, knowing that this shade is a danger and that one a protection, ventures a pace or stays as his hard-won knowledge bids him.

A cloud of such a size meant a shadow of such a duration. This cloud will carry one across the lawn, and when it has passed, the trees yonder will be won and their desired shade. From the south another cloud was coming, bulky as a two-acre field and buoyant as a gossamer. Folded in its gloom the wall could be crossed and the shelter of trees or of long grass reached before the moon came riding, delicately, in a radiance that was one half silver and one half blue.

So she fled. The lark watching from a dew-drenched covert was not more discreet as it turned again to the slumber that she had broken; and when she took the wall the bat that whirled from it made more noise than she did.

At times, when there was neither light nor dark, a world of grey and purple that was thirty feet high and fifteen feet around enclosed her in. And she stretched her ears towards the bounds of that small universe before she ventured another step.

Wonderful and terrifying were these dim oases of vision; and across them, coming from no place and dallying a moment ere

they went on to nowhere, more silent than
the night itself and as incomprehensible,
grey moths were flitting; dim as ghosts
they were, and as aloof; beating a tireless
gauze on no errand, tacking back and forth,
and disappearing in one flirt of a noiseless
wing. Small creatures seemed to wait until
her foot must fall on them, and then, with a
sound that lasted for two long seconds of
panic, they were gone; they disappeared,
and the world was utterly empty of them.
At these sounds she stood, her heart beating
up at her thoat and a sense of angry despair
flooding over and about her. Then she
moved again; slipping into and out of
shadows as featly as the moonbeam slipped
into and out of a cloud.

She knew where she was going, but not
what she was going to do. She would see
him again because she must, and after that,
if there was more to be done the time to do it
would bring the doing. But the one large
apprehension was as yet sufficient for her
mind—that she would see him again, and
that they would talk together. She was
sure that this time he would speak to her,
and that whatever he said would be wiser

and sweeter and stranger than any words she had yet listened to; and she wondered, without thought, what his magical utterance would mean and how it could possibly be replied to; knowing yet that her replies were already formed and that the only word she need utter until she died was the word " yes."

CHAPTER XVI

SHE stood again behind a tree, looking on
the camp-fire and the three figures that
stretched or moved about it. She listened,
but now without joy, to the babel of laughter
which sped between them. Back and forth
it went, endless, tireless. Youth calling and
answering to youth; catching a facile fire
from each other, and tossing it back as
carelessly. Spendthrift they were as young
gods; care-free as young animals; with
minds untroubled because they need not
work, and bodies that were at ease because
they were active; scorning the darkness in
a gaiety that was delicious because it was
thoughtless; and with a thoughtlessness
that was lovely because it was young. But,
to her, watching, listening, waiting, all that

merriment was a torment. She was their peer in youth and activity, but she was their superior in that she was thoughtful, for desire is thought not yet translated, and her desire would swell about the world and banish all else from existence so that she could fashion the regal solitude in which so gigantic a mystery might be contemplated.

Why, she thought frowningly, did these children not go to sleep. And why, she wondered, should older people submit to annoyance or be forced to await any young person's convenience?

But the night was advanced, and young people will sleep. Soon they stretched about the fire, and each composed himself to the slumber which comes as deliciously in its season as waking does; and, for their life favoured it, they fell into sleep as precipitately as though they were falling down a cliff.

She could scarcely wait for the five minutes that was required. Then she plucked a scrap of moss and tossed it on Naoise's breast.

As he fell asleep so he sprang awake:

he went dead asleep: he came wide awake, with every faculty alert, and his limbs as composed for movement as for rest. He saw the scrap of moss lying on his bosom, and, knowing that such things do not travel of their own accord, he looked for the cause, searching keenly among the boles that stretched in endless gleam and gloom about them.

She stood forward a pace.

Had she really moved, or was she impelled! Surely a hand had taken her by the shoulder and pushed her forward! But in the moment that she moved panic seized her as suddenly and overwhelmingly as a hawk swoops upon a mouse. She lifted a hand to her breast so that her heart might not be snatched away, but the hand went on to her lips and covered them in terror lest they should call. She turned with one swift and flying gesture, but the foot that aimed for flight continued its motion, and the full circle held her again facing the terror. For he had already risen, lithe as a cat and as noiseless, and in three great strides he was standing beside her, standing over her, encompassing her about; not now to be retreated from or escaped from or eluded in any way.

And as her heart had leaped so his leaped also, and they stood in an internal tumult, so loud, so intimate and violent that the uproar and rush of a storm was quietude in the comparison.

They could not speak. There were no words left in the world. There were only eyes that plunged into and fled from each other, and a mighty hand that had gripped her arm and would never release it again. A hand that pushed her backwards and backwards, away from the friendly logs that crackled and flamed; away from the quiet forms that might have rescued her but that lay as though slumbering in stone. She might have escaped with one sound, but the law of her being was that she must not make a sound. She might have escaped by just a show of reluctance; one small opposition, nay, hesitation, to the pressure of that hand. But she would not make that infinitesimal wraith of motion. A weariness as of piled worlds went from his finger to her mind, and it was forbidden her to have any longer an initiative. A lethargy that was utter surrender stole into her limbs. She did not think, she did not desire: she was as void of speculation as though she were dead; and while his hand continued to guide she would go, and when it ceased she would no longer be capable of either movement or repose.

All fear of interruption had passed, and yet they went on cautiously, noiselessly, as though interruption was imminent or unescapable; putting trees and yet more trees between them and the leaping fire; striving to forget the fire; seeking a more involved darkness, and finding everywhere a gloom that yet revealed them. They could not discover darkness. They could not get to a place where they could cease to see each other. Always it looked black farther on, and always when they got there they could each see the pale confronting face of the other, with the darkness everywhere but in those faces.

They stopped perforce, with that feeling of tremendous discouragement wherein passion sinks back upon itself, where desire ceases and nothing is instant but weariness. His hand yet held her, but it gripped no longer: it lay on her arm as a dead weight:

she had only to move an inch and it would fall away: she had but to turn and he would not follow her even with his eyes; but the energy which had drained from him flooded into her in one whirling stream, and when his hand fell away hers took up the duty it relinquished.

CHAPTER XVII

IF Lavarcham had ever permitted herself excitement she would have been excited the next day. But there is a curious means by which we may postpone the spending of our emotions. There are many people who can only do a particular thing on condition that they do it in two directions. They can repress themselves only when they are engaged in repressing some one else; for the thing we are doing outwardly and to others is always the thing that we are doing inwardly and to ourselves. If we treat others benevolently we are assuredly being kind to ourselves: if we mete out torment we will receive that measure and will writhe in it. A tyrant is ultimately one who is striving for self-mastery by the wrong method. But in order to be good you must do good, or to be anything you must do that thing concretely, for life is movement and all else is movement too.   Lavarcham by unconscious processes discovered that Deirdre needed the utmost disciplinary and repressive measures that could be applied to a human being.

"The child is running wild," she complained to the air that circulated about Deirdre's head.

"But I have not done a thing," cried Deirdre.

"There are a thousand things you should have done," Lavarcham replied.

"What are they?" Deirdre demanded.

But Lavarcham did not know.

She certainly felt within herself the necessity for doing a thousand things.   She felt so busy that there must really be a thousand things to be done.   But she knew also that nothing remained for her to do, and, consequently, that Deirdre was to blame.

The real thing she had to do was to master her own excitement, and she perceived at a glance that Deirdre was in a very excited condition indeed.

"You must sit quietly, my treasure," she

counselled. "You must not move from one place to another, taking things up and putting them down. You will become fidgetty yourself and will give every one about you the fidgets also."

"But——" Deirdre expostulated.

"And you must not give back-answers. When you are told to do a thing you must do it cheerfully and patiently——"

"But——" cried Deirdre.

"For," Lavarcham continued, "lacking this self-control and gentleness of movement no girl can become a lady."

"But," Deirdre exploded, "I have not done a thing."

"You know, my one treasure, that everything I say is for your good, and when I counsel you it is because I consider you need just that counsel. You are distraught to-day, my bud of the branch, and there is no reason why you should not be as calm to-day as you were yesterday or any day. This is only to-day, but to-morrow will come and to-day will be forgotten."

"I do not understand in the least——" Deirdre began.

"There is nothing to understand, my

beloved. There is not a reason in the world that you should be troubled. Sit now at your embroidery, and do not leave it until I give permission."

Deirdre was indeed excited, but Lavarcham had not the smallest perception of this: nor was it visible. It was a very intimate excitement, which could be brooded and enjoyed as well over a piece of embroidery as in any other way. And Lavarcham watched her, sensing nothing of that deep agitation and memory and dream.

I was wise, she thought, not to tell the news, for the child seems even more beautiful to-day than she has ever seemed before. She has slept well.

While they were thus sitting a servant hurried into the room, with her eyes bolting from her head, and a gabble on her lips which Lavarcham only repressed by ferocity, for she surmised at once that the king had arrived, and she did not even yet wish Deirdre to know of the visit.

She rose and precipitated herself against the servant.

"Is that how you enter a room, ill-bred slave? Was it among the cattle that you

learned manners? Begone at once," she
cried, "and do not come into a room again
until you have asked and received permission
to enter. What is the world coming to?" she
continued angrily as she hustled the servant
through the door and down the corridor.

"It's the son of Ness——" the servant
babbled.

"And if it is," said Lavarcham, "there
is the more reason for you to be attentive
and respectful and unseen. Go to your
place and stay there until I send for you."

She returned then, and, still simulating
ill-temper, she dismissed Deirdre to her
own room.

"You have not properly trimmed your
finger-nails," she scolded; "there is a
black spot under one of them. You are
not seemly. Go to your room at once, little
blossom, and when you come back come so
that your fosterer need not be ashamed of
her charge."

Saying so she marched Deirdre to her
room and thrust her in. Then she returned,
and, seating herself at the embroidery from
which she had driven her ward, she prepared to receive the king.

CHAPTER XVIII

"WELL, my heart," said the king, as he strode through the door of the Sunny Chamber.

With a keen glance he took in all that was to be seen. The woodwork of the walls and floors that were polished and polished again until they shone like crystal. The great carved chairs, each placed at the same prim distance from the other and from the wall; and the skins and furs that formed geometrical patterns and gradations of colour on the floor.

Conachúr shook his head as he regarded.

"Methodical," he said, as he sat down.

"Orderly, master," she corrected gently.

"It is a woman's room," he insisted. "No man could live in it."

"No man does," said the humble dame.

"And by merely entering I have ruined it already," the king continued in a grievous tone; "I have kicked three rugs out of alignment," he said ruefully.

"It is a small matter," said Lavarcham.

"I am certain that your heart is ill at ease, and although your hands are folded they are twitching to restore these rugs; rearrange them if you must, my good friend."

"If the king permits me," she cried joyfully, and with a few deft touches she replaced the rugs.

"You may sit down," said the king. "And now, where is this baby you deafen the world about?"

Lavarcham clapped her hands, and, to the servant who appeared in the doorway—

"Tell your mistress, Deirdre, that she is required immediately—and do not tell her that a visitor is with me or woe betide you."

The servant disappeared.

Conachúr looked at her quizzically.

"The girl does not know that I was coming?"

Lavarcham pursed her lips.

"I have not mentioned it to her."

The king, with his elbow on his knee, continued to regard her mockingly.

"Is it that you are careful or careless, my friend?"

"I am careful, master. I am always careful," she replied.

"But," he continued gently, "she will not be apparelled so as to be looked on by a visitor."

"She will be seen as she would be seen any hour of any day, and thus it will be known, master, that Lavarcham does her duty."

"You are the wonder of Emania," said Conachúr. "I hear a step," he continued, and, removing his elbow from his knee, he stretched out a great leg and turned towards the door.

Deirdre entered like a whirlwind of legs and laughter, and, seeing a huge man staring at her, she halted as if she had been stopped by a wall, whirled about and would have vanished again but that Lavarcham's voice restrained her.

"The king has come to visit us, my pulse," said the suave Lavarcham.

The blood pounded into Deirdre's heart

and into her temples; for an instant her
body seemed to be filled with noise and
blindness, and in the next instant the lady,
trained for every emergency and in every
etiquette, was mistress again. Deirdre advanced, made a great reverence, and knelt at
the king's knee.

He gave her his hand to kiss.

"You may rise, my fawn," said the
monarch.

She arose and stood with downcast eyes.
She did not dare to look at him. All that
came within her vision was a mighty leg
draped in green silk, from which long
tassels of gold swung gently. The king
stared narrowly at her, and Lavarcham
stared narrowly at the king.

"Go now, my dear," said Lavarcham,
"and see that refreshments are brought for
the king."

Deirdre again made her deep reverence,
and, on rising, her hasty upward glance
was caught by Conachúr's eye. She trod
swiftly backwards, staring, and it was with
parted lips and wide eyes that she disappeared from the room.

But the king continued staring at the

doorway like one who has seen a vision and is striving with every fibre to recreate that which has vanished.

"Was I not right, master?" said Lavarcham gently.

"She is the Bud of the Branch," said Conachúr. "She is the Fragrant Apple of the Bough."

"Did I not say that she was beautiful?" cried the gleeful and vehement lady.

"You did not say so," he replied sternly. "You never told me of this."

"Nay, master, you would not believe me."

"It could not be told," the thoughtful monarch admitted. "If the flight of the swallow could be imparted by words, or the crisping of foam: if the breath of the lily could be uttered, or the beauty of a young tree on a sunny hill: then this Troubler might be spoken of. Have you noticed, my friend, how the sun paints glories and wonders on the sky as he goes west in the evening, or at early morn with what noble tenderness he comes again: she is radiant and tender as the sun, Lavarcham."

"Thus it is," said Lavarcham.

"She is nine times sweeter than the

cuckoo on the branch," he cried. "I give her the Pass before all the women of the world, for she is notable and delicate and dear."

"Then you will marry her as is fitting," Lavarcham pleaded. "You will not give my baby to a rough gentleman."

The king stood furiously from his chair.

"She is for no man but the king," he stormed. "She shall be my one wife until Doom."

CHAPTER XIX

In ten seconds the floor rugs had sailed from
their anchorages and were lying some neatly
inside out and all in woeful askewness. The
chairs left their military formation; some
stood seat to seat like couples preparing for
a dance, others in the woeful, slack isolation
of those who stare after uncivil partners that
have fled. And in this wreckage of a woman's
room Conachúr strode.

"Lavarcham," he cried, "there shall
be great deeds done in Ireland from this
day."

"Yes, my dear lord."

"I am twenty years younger than I was
an hour ago. I could leap like a young
buck, Lavarcham."

"Yes, my dear lord," she stammered.

"Poets shall sing more wisely in Eirè

because of this day; harpers shall play more sweetly; the magicians shall win increase of power, for through me this land shall be possessed by power and beauty."

"Yes, my sweet lord," cried the transformed woman.

"You shall be with me always, Lavarcham."

"Oh, my master!"

"I shall marry thee to an hero, and thy descendants for ever shall sit, even in the presence of a king."

"Nay, I shall kneel, and all my seed shall kneel in the house of my dear lord."

"Sit down, my soul, and let us talk. Lavarcham," he said, "that girl shall be my wife."

"I have dreamed of this day," she murmured.

"You knew I would marry her?"

"I knew that my lord loves the best, and that she is the best. I trained her for my lord."

"She is the best," he conceded. "She is better than the best."

"The king will never blush for his bride, nor I for my training," she continued, "for in everything that becomes a lady she is well taught."

"So!" said Conachúr.

"There is no ceremony of court or camp that she does not understand. There is no domestic care that she is not mistress of. She can touch the harp like a master, she can make a poem like a bard."

"You give me pleasure, Lavarcham, but all these she need do or not do as she pleases. Tell me rather of herself, what is her mode? What is her way of thinking?"

"She is loving and obedient as a pet fawn, and she is wild-spirited as a wild fawn. She is thoughtful for others; she loves knowledge, and she fears nothing."

"Even lacking all this, there is yet the makings of a queen in her."

Lavarcham nodded a satisfied head.

"But she does not lack, and she is a queen. In a week, when she has become used to the crowd and the court, all the others will fall back to their own places and she will remain in her place."

"I think it will be so. But," and he aroused again, "you have said nothing about the curve of her cheek, Lavarcham."

"What would a poor woman say of that!"
she cried gleefully.

"I saw her neck when she bent over my
hand, and I saw the two great tresses falling
away on either side. Lavarcham, that was
a wonder to see!"

"We see with our own sight, master."

"When she stood up I saw the lips that
had touched my hand: and I looked in her
eyes as she went away. There is no end to
those depths of light, and I can imagine that
they would change as the deep sea changes.
If she were angry they would be—thus; and
if she smiled they would be thus again; the
same and different. If she smiled her lips
would move in the smile. How do her lips
go when they smile, Lavarcham?"

"These are things which women are
blind to, master; they are seen only by
men. You must ask your poets to tell of
them for this is man's talk, and no woman is
versed in it."

"Lavarcham!"

"Yes, master!"

"I shall take her away with me this day."

"Master!"

"Bring her to the Red Branch at nightfall."

118

"Master!"

"At nightfall, you hear me."

"I will not do it."

"What will you not do, slave, that I order?"

"I will not debauch your queen."

"Lavercham——!"

"No one shall make a leman of my babe."

"She shall return in a few hours. Be with her at the Red Branch to-night. Do not fail on your life."

"If I bring her my knife will be in her bosom."

Conachúr leaned back in his chair and the terrible staring frown went from his face.

"We shall certainly marry Lavarcham to an hero. I am impatient, my heart, but strength and victory lies always with the one who can abide, and I can, even in torment. Have your way, woman."

"It is the best way, master. You shall thank me yet for this way."

He smiled wryly.

"Dear, my lord," she continued earnestly, "there must be the ceremonies that befit a king's wedding, and guests must be

invited from the four great Provinces of
Ireland. It cannot all be done before two
little months."

"You shall have one week, my friend."

"A week! O my master!"

"A woman's mind runs to gauds and
tricks and rites, but in a week we two shall
be married, and you may have ceremonies
for a year afterwards if you wish for them."

Lavarcham wrung her hands.

"O my sweet lord——"

"It shall be so," said the king.

Lavarcham sat dumb.

"In this house," he continued impatiently,
"refreshments are long in appearing, and
after those excitements and battlings we
need them."

"They only wait permission to enter,"
she stammered, and clapped her hands.

Deirdre appeared with three servants
carrying silver trays. She took one and
knelt to present it to the king.

"Nay, you shall partake with me, and
Lavarcham shall serve us. Let those others
go."

At a sign from Lavarcham the servants

placed their trays on tables and retired with terrified courtesies.

"Taste from the cup, my brightness," said Conachúr, "and afterwards I shall taste."

"A Rí Uasal!" Deirdre stammered.

"All precedence is yours from this hour. Are you not called the Troubler?"

"I am, lord."

"You have troubled the king, O sky-woman. Do not be shy with me or frightened, for although a king is terrible to all he is not fearful to a queen. Drink from my cup, O queen."

Deirdre glanced hastily towards Lavarcham, for this conversation had taken a turn which her training had not provided for, but her guardian was sitting bemused, in a trance of benevolence and admiration.

She sipped from the cup, and, with a tiny smile of apology and fear, tendered it again to the staring king. He took the vessel, and her hand with it.

"I imagined it so," he said, "I imagined how the thin red lip would arch and curve and cling to the cup; and I foresaw how it would cling and uncurve and re-arch and withdraw. The poets tell of such wonders when they can, but I know these things by my own virtue better than they do. One day, O shy cluster of delight, you will sing to me: my harper shall listen to that when I can bear a companion, for I may grudge a sight or a sound of you even to the men of art. I shall see your hair done otherwise, and this way again. I shall see you stir about me, this side and that and backwards; a thousand harmonies of movement that I divine and a thousand that I know nothing of. Do not be fearful, O little twisted loop of the ringlets, for you are my beloved. You shall have no weariness or lack for ever, for I shall fold you in my affection as a hawk folds air within her wings. You shall leave these bleak halls and yon mangy field to sit at the banquets in the Red Branch: to be the Queen of Ulster, the pearl of the world, and my own heart's comrade."

Deirdre was the more alarmed, not only because a strange and mighty gentleman was holding a strange and monstrous discourse to her, but he was holding her hand, and she did not know how to retrieve it. She thought it would not be polite to laugh, although she vastly wanted to, and she knew it would be foolish to cry, although she was so bewildered and terrified that an ocean of frightened tears was surging behind her eyes.

"Lavarcham, my sweet mother," she murmured in distress.

And that low plaint went to Conachúr's heart like a sword of delight, so that his soul was shaken and he could have wept for pity and love.

"Return to your embroidery, my child," said Lavarcham. "I shall come to you later and prepare your mind for all that is in store for you."

Deirdre stood up then and fled, only remembering her courtesy at the doorway.

CHAPTER XX

LAVERCHAM came to her as promised, and she told Deirdre for hours of the delights to come.

"In a week," she said, "you will be gone from here, and our home will be desolate indeed. But although the king called this a bleak den, and spoke of our demesne as a mangy field, he was not right in doing so. A house is bleak that has no children running and shouting in it, and this house will be bleak when you are gone; but in all other respects a cleaner or better appointed dwelling will not be found in the Five Great Fifths of Ireland; mark me well, child, the king was excited and unjust, and I shall tell him so. When you rule in Emania you will find how difficult it is to keep all things in order, and how hard it is to have even one

room clean; for men will be stirring at all
hours of the day and night in your palace, and
although they can make a home in a field men
make nothing but dirt in a house.

"You will have much to do and to remember, my secret bud, but, above all, you must
remember the genealogies of Ireland and the
precedences of the court as I have taught
them to you, and in any doubt or dispute
ask me rather than the herald. The chief
cause of trouble in a country is the herald,
for he is always wrong, and even when he is
right in fact he is wrong in tact. Do not
take any other woman's counsel in those
matters; do not even seek it—the one wish
of all women is to advance their husbands,
and themselves by consequence, and they
will ruin the world if they are let.

"Do not forget that, after the king, the
first man in the land is Fergus the son of
Roy. Be quick in respect to him, but be
slow to sit by him or to talk with him, for
Conachúr loves him on the surface, but he
hates him in the bone. The first woman in
the land is the wife of Fergus, the king's
mother. Be obedient to Ness in everything. Be quick in your courtesies to her.

125

Give her many kisses. Be careful not to love her, for her love is uncertain as a cat's paw, and where she strikes she draws blood. But these two are not often at Emania. They live in their fortress, deep in love, or in thought, as Conachúr fancies.

"You will see Findcheam, the wife of Amargin the Wonderful, and Dervorgilla, wife of Lugad of the Red Stripes, Fedelm-of-the-Fresh-Heart, the wife of Laerí the Victorious, and Niab, the daughter of Celt-char mac Uthecar, and Brig Brethach, his wife. Hussies all! spit-fires and scratch-cats! There is Lendubair, Conall Cearnach's wife, and Findige, wife of Eogan mac Durthacht, and Fedelm-of-the-Nine Shapes, the king's daughter. They, and an hundred others. You will meet them all.

"They have all been whispering of you this year back: and they have told more lies of you than will be told again until you die. You will like them at first, for many of them are nearly of your age, and they will fuss and gallop and chatter about you like daws. Give them all the listening you like, give them all the kisses they will take—Oh, you will be kissed from morning to night, my pet—but do not give one of them a moment's confidence.

"The king will talk to you urgently, whispering in your ear like a madman. There is nothing he will not tell you in the night, however deep it is, or hidden; for a man in love will give all that he has to the beloved; he would give his soul if he knew how to do it; and Conachúr will think that by telling all his secrets to you he will somehow tell all your secrets to himself. Men are so. But that which he tells must be uttered to no other ear, for what is whispered in the palace will be shouted down the Boyne. You can tell me all, for I am different; I am your nurse, your mother, and your one friend, but to no other person must you shape even one syllable.

"When the king has confided to you all that he can think of he will beg you to confide in him: he will pray you to tell him all that you have even done or thought—when he tells you of the wild glees and savageries of love tell him in return of how you feed your pet fawn; for a man, and the gods know why, delights to think that his beloved has a fawn in the valley, and he will listen for ever

to the tale of how it is fed and of its grateful
eyes.

"You will meet many men in the palace,
and each gentleman that you speak to will
be looked at closely by the king.   Until this
day he has been aware of women as one is
aware of the sun, but now he will grow aware
of men as one is aware of a wound.   You
will not see him look, but look he will; and
when you seem most free from observation
he will be studying you.   Whether it be a
captain or a butler that your eyes rest on, he
will know, without looking, at whom you
are looking, and thereafter he will examine
that person for himself, and he will examine
you in curious ways about that person.   Any
question he ever asks about a man will be a
trap for you.   Answer him carelessly about
them all, and make the same answer about
them all.

"It is safe to say of all men that they are
nice, but do not say that one is nicer than
another.   There is no end to the windings
of his mind, and if you say that one man is
ugly and another not he will dream about
the distinction and will dream you terribly
into his dream.   A dreaming man is magical,

128

for he will make the dream come true against his own wish and interest, and Conachúr is at the age to have those dreams.

"Be gentle and uncertain with him.   Be wild and coy.   Do not, although he prays you, be familiar with him.   Tire quickly of dalliance, for in middle life a man likes not to think that he has wearied first.   Dance often but do not gambol.   Be girlish but not childish.   Do not pluck his beard or tickle him.   Sit sparingly on his knee.   It is only old men who like baby tricks, and he is not, by fifteen years, old enough for that.

"Discuss your dresses and ornaments with him: ask his advice about your ribbons; he will laugh at you and chide you, but he will love that to be done, and he will love you for doing it.   Should he be sportive among women, pout then a little, make a small lament, but take no heed of it.   He has outlived all the chances of desire.

"He will love you only, and each day he will love you more.   What fear there is will be on his side; he will be afraid of men; and there your heed must be endless, for you must not hurt the king even by a second's thoughtlessness.   His equal is not in Eirè for majesty and wisdom.   He is a great king, a great man, a royal hero.   O my lamb! all that is of good luck and of noble fate has come to you, and you should thank the king for ever on your knees, and thank your poor Lavarcham who planned this happiness."

CHAPTER XXI

AND Conachúr lived anew as he drove home-wards.

He did not see the humble people who louted and stared as he dashed by, nor the others who stood at strict attention marvelling at a king who returned no salute.

His feet were so light he could have bounded in the chariot, but his heart was lighter still.

It flew into his brain and stayed there, buoyant as a bubble, creative as a moon; so charging his mind with its own essence that all which was material merged in a flash to the spirit. The earth was eased of grossness and became a shimmer of colours and trans-parencies; an aura of gold and green rose on the crests of the manifolding hills. The tender involutions of no bird's song was

131

heard, for all songs merged into that of the lyrical earth and the clouds and the shining spaces between them. The world was singing for Conachúr, and he was song. For to the clairvoyance of love all that is unseen takes on sweet shape, and all that we see we are shapen to. A new world emerges softly from the old: not imperceptibly and un-reckoned, but by such divine gradations as we may note and rejoice in. Then the creator is manifest in his creation, and all in us. We are it and all: we are the soul of the world, and our own soul: we are the victors, for we are beyond fear: we are the masters, for we are beyond desire.

How should fear or lust reach to the tops we spurn! The sour-faced beggar shaking his oaken bowl may have our purse and a clasp of the hand to boot. Yon shaking anatomy that hovers and limps shall have our own health if none other is at hand, for all now is soft and easy, and at one bend of a brow the Land of Heart's Desire may be in being.

So Conachúr went, dreaming; the shaper of a world that was malleable to his wish.

To this hour he had triumphed in all that

132

he had undertaken, but he had been unfriended, forging alone as in granite all that he willed, and feeling at every instant the rigour of life and the intractability of events. He saw that nothing he had yet done was so completed that it might be forgotten.   Here an event had left dissatisfaction in its wake: there it had left an enemy.   But from henceforth his work would have the clean finish of the spring, and all that he planted should grow from the root.

He would have double strength; his titanic own, and hers, breathing in him like an elixir, exciting him, heartening him.   She was—what was she not!   She was his tomorrow.   She was his all and his last chance. She was his future, vivifying all that had grown stale, and unfolding horizons where an uttermost end had seemed.   For at times an ending comes on every man, and thereafter there is nothing to strive for, there being nothing left to hope for; energy winces from the thought of any task, and the future but prolongs a present that is insipid and wearisome.

The departure of Maeve had been such an ending for Conachúr.   Life had halted there

for him, or had moved in a round of sameness
which chafed and tormented his whirling
mind.   But he could forget her now and
start afresh, for when he looked on Deirdre
she went into his blood and into his bones, so
that to be removed from her was as though
he were distant from his own arms or his own
head.

He was impatient, and wished that all
should know, as at one shout, his glorious
news, but he yet would not speak of it to
any one.   He knew that he might safely
leave the publishing of that event to Lavarcham, and that ere nightfall every house in a
radius of twenty miles would be talking of
the king's marriage.

Down every road that ran from Emain
Macha messengers would be going in swift
chariots to tell the tale and to bid those who
were worthy to the wedding feast. Not
stopping for more than a few minutes at any
place; changing horses at the guest-houses,
and dashing off again; some deep into
Connacht in the west, others eastwards into
Leinster, and more again speeding the long
centre of Ireland to the two Munsters.
These distant kings and princes would think

they had been slighted by such short notice, or by a notice that could only reach them after the event. But his wedding feast should endure for three months, and there would be pleasure and leisure for all. At this moment, if Lavarcham was doing her duty (and she was never neglectful), the ostlers should be pulling the great chariots out and backing the snorting horses between the shafts.

To-morrow would be a new day.

Every person who observed the king would look on him with something else in the regard. Many reserves would be down, many barriers broken: for all people look differently on the king when he is in love, and they try to bathe in his fortunate regard.

The men would glance at him shyly and subtly: each look a reminder and a well-wishing. While he stood among them he and they would laugh without any word being said, and they would be more familiar with him than they would otherwise dare. But if one dared to clap his shoulder, Conachúr would clap that comrade's shoulder again.

The women would look at him more

135

openly; more softly and broodingly; each
mutely assuring him that all which was to
come would be good; each telling him that
woman guards for man all that which no
man can give; each telling that because he
loved one woman he must love all, and that
women are truly lovable, and are precious
beyond all precious things.   He would see
that they all wished to touch him, so that he
might know they were truly woman and not
different from her he delighted in; and he
would see them turn from him, humbled and
aggrieved, seeking anxiously in other eyes
for the confirmations which he must not
give.

For when the king is in love the world
goes mad, and all who love him must cherish
each other or sicken of their suppressed
loyalty and adoration.

For weeks to come Ulster would be an
orgy.   The man who had dodged marriage
as a fox tricks the hen-wife would tumble
into it with a thud: those who craved for and
feared it would find that they were married
in a morning: maids would become daring
and men shy.   From one, walking coyly in
the moonlight, a shoulder-band might slip,

and the moon and a man would be rewarded for being out at night.   One who stood and spoke might suddenly shape her lips thus, and the man who looked would go blind in his brains and stay so to the last quarter of the moon.   A wave of frolic and daring would go from the king, and thrill to the last hamlet in his kingdom; for although war is glorious, death is its ruler and companion; but from love life flows and everything that is lovely.

And, as his heart rose thus, Conachúr knew that he was the life of his people, for he was king and lover, and that all swung about him as the world swings round the sun.

CHAPTER XXII

BUT for Deirdre a night went by which to
the end of her days she would not care to
remember.

She had seen the king at last: that being,
all memory and dream, half monster and
half baby, whom she remembered from
Lavarcham's endless tale. She had seen
the grave brow, the graver eyes, the bushy,
reddish-yellow hair looped back to the slope
of his poll, and the yellow beard cleft at the
centre and foaming in two points to the
breast. She could not have thought that a
man might be so huge, so steady, so master-
ful. He was a being to whom one might
pray, or for whom one might die joyfully.
If a lord came striding from the Shí surely
he would look as Conachúr did: massive
and dazzling and wonderful; with an eye

from which one winced as from the sun, and with a voice that trolled and astonished like the note of a beaten drum. She remembered his hand that could hold both of her own with ease, and the great ridge of his shoulders, sloping away like the easy run and fall of a mountain.

And this terrific being claimed her as his wife!

Nothing but terror filled her heart at that prospect, for she could not see him in any terms of intimacy or affection. He was and would remain as remote as her childhood, and no mere nearness could make him present. And he would be as unaccountable as are the elements that smile to-day and rage to-morrow in hurricane. What woman could reckon his parts or his total? He was like some god that had come out of the hills to astonish and terrify.

And there was Naoise!

As her memory retrieved the beloved name her heart went bustling to her throat, and she sat raging and terrified.

It was not that he would be defrauded of her: it would be his own business to be woeful on that count; but she would be

defrauded of him, and her proper lack was
as yet sufficient for her mood, for lacking him
what could be returned to her? Her hands
went cold and her mouth dry as she faced
such a prospect.

The youth who was hers! Who had no
terrors for her! Who was her equal in
years and frolic! She could laugh with
him, and at him. She could chide him and
love him. She could give to him and with-
hold. She could be his mother as well as
his wife. She could annoy him and forgive
him. For between them there was such an
equality of time and rights that neither could
dream of mastery or feel a grief against the
other. He was her beloved, her comrade,
the very red of her heart, and her choice
choice.

Deirdre leaped from the bed, but she could
not leap from her thoughts, and she could
not attempt the crazy and mazy corridors of
her home to fly to him; for the excited household was clattering and chattering in the
corridors, and she could no more escape by
them than a bird can escape by its cage.

It was not until two nights had passed
that she could dare the wall; and in the

intervening days she must listen to Lavarcham, endless in caution and advice.

Do this, but do not on your life do that.
Remember this always, and this and this and
this. There seemed as much to remember
not to forget as there was to remember to
remember.

Deirdre would turn an eye on her guardian
so lack-lustre at times, and again so woeful
or wild, that the good lady marvelled.

"Do not be frightened, my silk of the
flock," her guardian soothed, "there is
every cause for joy and none for fear. In
three days you will be the most envied lady
in Ulster, and in four you will be the happi-
est. Tell Lavarcham what is in your mind
and what you are afraid of?"

"I am in dread of the king," said Deirdre.

"That will pass," Lavarcham advised,
"and in a few days you will wonder that
you could have been frightened. But a
maid is a maid: all that she thinks or dreams
is founded on inexperience, and has nothing
to do with reality: the world pours into a
young girl's lap heedless of what she wished
or dreaded; for no person can either hope
or fear until they know actually that which

is hopeful or frightful. All you need do is to accept what your heart approves of, and what your heart rejects you can throw away. There is everything to hope for and nothing to be afraid of."

But her chance did come at last.

She found the sons of Uisneac still at their encampment, but they were a silent trio. They were more than silent: they were abashed and embarrassed.

"What is it?" Deirdre murmured, feeling the constraint.

"We are bidden to your wedding," said Naoise shyly.

The mild candour of his voice went into her heart like a sword, so that she could not speak to him, and it was to his brother she turned.

"What shall we do, dear Ainnle?" she asked.

But he had no answer for her, and it was the youngest who replied.

"Let us all run away," Ardan cried, and his face went suddenly red and his eager eyes shone like stars.

Naoise glanced at Deirdre from under his brows.

"Where could we run to from the king?" Ainnle grumbled impatiently.

"And we do not come of a race that run away," said Naoise.

Silence fell. But the statement of his own quality had unlocked a door of bitterness in Naoise's heart.

"Nor will you easily find the girl who will run away from a kingdom," he continued as though addressing reasonable counsel to his juniors.

Deirdre faced him gravely and lovingly.

"I will run away with you," she said.

"The king——!" Naoise gasped.

"I am afraid of that king," she whispered urgently.

But her lover was pale and terrified.

It would be an affront that was never offered to a king in Eirè. It would be a cruelty: it would be an awful deed.

He turned to his brothers. "The king is our uncle, he loves us," he said.

"Yes," Ainnle agreed, "he loves us better than his own sons."

"After Cúchulinn," said Ardan, "he loves us best in the world."

"And he loves me," said Deirdre.

143

Naoise leaped to his feet.

"O gods of day and night!" he cried.

He seemed to plead to Deirdre for comprehension and pity.

"Conachúr reared me like his own son: I sat in his lap: he buckled this sword on me with his own hand, he put his two palms on my shoulders when I won my weapons, and he kissed me three times on each cheek. I love and venerate him."

Again silence throbbed among them.

"I shall go home to Lavarcham," said Deirdre.

The boys looked at her and at each other and at the ground and did not know where to look any more.

"I also shall be reared by the son of Ness," she said gently. "I too shall sit in his lap. He will not buckle a sword on me, but he will unbuckle my girdle with his own hands; he will put his two palms on my shoulders, and he will kiss me many times on each cheek."

Naoise beat a fist against his brow.

"I am the king's man," he stammered.

But she turned her fleet smile and trembling lips on him.

"Am I to tell the king how well we loved each other, night after night among the trees? or would it be better to keep that as a secret among us four: they say that men can keep secrets."

The two lads blushed painfully and turned away.

Naoise was as one who has renounced life.

"There is nothing to be done," said his dry lips. And then, shaking his shoulders, he tossed care from them.

"We shall be beyond the trees at this hour to-morrow night with the chariots," he said. "If the hour passes and you do not come we shall attack the guards and take you out."

He turned to the others.

"You must come with us, wherever we go, my brothers, for when the king finds that I am gone he will slay you two for eric."

"He wouldn't kill me," Ardan boasted, "for I wouldn't let him."

"Nobody but Cúchulinn could kill you," Ainnle scoffed.

"You couldn't, anyway," the youngest retorted.

"Little boasting Pillar of Combat!" his
brother gibed.   "Pooh!   Battle-Torch of
the Gael!"

And in terrified merriment they made the
rest of their arrangements.

CHAPTER XXIII

LAVARCHAM left the king's presence.

She came away bowed and blind and dizzy, shuffling in any direction and unaware of why she was walking or where she was going. An hundred thoughts, battling furiously for precedence, kept her thoughtless; an hundred pictures, each striving for place and examination, kept her blind. She was all a din and whirl and swirl, as though the winds that raged in gust and countercurrent through her brain were blowing her along. At times she would remember that she did not wish to go where she was going, and she would spin furiously aside and go as stupidly in another path; and at times she would discover that she was standing, still and collected as a stone, a nothing; staring on nothing. Great sighs broke from her

147

miserable heart; or she was so shattered
by dry sobbings that it seemed her bones
must part company with her flesh and with
each other: and again, with her two hands
gripped on her mouth she squeezed back a
medley of screams, and listened, as in amazement, to the thin whinings that forced
through the crooked spaces in her fingers.
Again, the cautious woman would peep
and peer to see if any person was nigh to
observe her, and before that survey could
make its round she would forget what she
was looking for, and think that *they* could
not be seen from this place, for they have
hours' start, and will be—where? by this
time.

With what unbelieving anguish that
flight had forced itself upon her! She
had gone trotting and ambling and panting
about her rooms and fields, calling—

"Deirdre, Deirdre, Deirdre?"

Searching for her baby in a work-basket
or on the flat of a ceiling, while the servants
gibbered and squealed and bubbled and
blared at her and at each other.

With what an iron dismay the thought
of Conachúr came on her, desolating and

unreckoned as the thunderclap which howls
on the heels of its howling brother.

He must be told.

And at that she poked up her nose like a
moonstruck dog pealing scream on scream,
until the attending hags fled into corners
as the mice do when they are frightened, and
screamed with her and at her and at the roof.

She went to Conachúr.

She stood mumbling and staring outside the
door and then trotted in, whispering at him:

"She's gone."

And Conachúr echoed, in uncomprehend-
ing amazement:

"She's gone."

Lavarcham stared into the king's face
that was carved in the granite of suspense
and astonishment.

"She's gone, little Deirdre's gone," she
yelled, and emptied her thin fingers on the
air as though she emptied them of Deirdre.
She clapped her hands together with a
dreadful giggle, and flapped her arms along
her thighs like some ungainly crow that has
been set dancing drunk on mead.

"When a maid goes a man goes with
her," she croaked.

149

She flopped to the door and hopped out of it and popped back.

"She's gone," she cried. "She's gone; she ran away with a man"; and she wobbled to the doorway again, nodding and tittering at the king until she disappeared.

The servants and guards were listening with their eyes staring, their mouths open, and their breathing forgotten.

A whisper, a thrill, a terrible constriction of the heart fled through the vast palace, and went zig-zagging like wildfire about Ulster. And in the centre of that Conachúr stood, alone; with his fists closed and his eyes closed; listening to the whispers that were an inch away and an hundred miles away; that were over him and under him and in him: listening to the blanching of his face and to the liquifying of his bones: listening in a rage of curiosity and woe for the more that might be said and all the more that might be thought: trying, as with one gripping of the mind, to sense all the bitterness that might be; to exhaust it in one gulp, and re-awaken as at a million removes from all that had ever been or could be till Doom.

BOOK II

CHAPTER I

TIME flies, scattering on all that had seemed
important the ash of forgetfulness, and so
crowding memory into memory that the
thing we recollect has no longer the shape
or colour that strode against us once upon
a time.

For all men but the dreamer time flies.
But it may be stationary for him who can
recreate in the night all that he forces to
oblivion in the morning. His woeful yester-
days can be timely at any time, for nothing
that touches him will rust or fade, and he
may be seen to wince at a word which his
contemporaries have lost the significance of.

The seven years that passed had not
touched Conachúr. He was still the master-
ful king, the unremitting lawgiver. He was
still the idol of his people. What would a

banquet in the Red Branch be if the king were away? But he was never absent, and wherever there was music or frolic or laughter the Son of Ness was urging it on, and would be eager for more when the youngest companion was wearied to stupidity. Not time nor thought could blunt the edge of his bodily or mental energy so vast was it, and misfortune beat as unavailingly against him as the wind did against oaken Emania.

To be energetic and self-sufficing is to be happy; but while one desire remains in the heart happiness may not come there. For to desire is to be incomplete: it is the badge of dependence, the signal of unhappiness, and to be freed from that is to be freed from every fetter that can possibly be forged. Man becomes god when he finds his satisfactions within himself, but his dreams then are other than those that harried Conachúr as a pack of hounds harry a fox.

For Ulster might forget, and those who had not been outraged might forgive, but he would not forget or forgive until he was as dead as those should be against whom his mind was directed like the point of a secret spear.

Deirdre and the sons of Uisneac had fled to Scotland, where they had kinsmen and acquaintances who had grown up with them in Emain Macha as fosterages from the Scottish courts, or as lords and captains in Conachúr's mercenary armies. They may have met Cúchulinn there, for it would be about that time that he was under the tuition of the female warrior and witch, Scatach; and, if so, they should have met his comrade Ferdiad also, he who was to assail the ford afterwards with what a hand! and it may have been during their exile that Cúchulinn fell in love with Scatach's daughter, and that the child was born who would receive such a woeful stroke on Báile's Strand.

It is one of the wise arrangements of providence that no person can either eat of the same thing or talk of the same thing for more than a week; and so, when gossip's time had passed, Ulster, unless it might be to some travelling historian, spoke no more of the king's misfortune. Such an historian would have learned that Deirdre was tall and short, and that she was dark and fair and

sallow: for every woman he interviewed
would lend her own contours and complexion to such an heroine, and would, as
they reprobated or forgave, endow her with
the moral qualities which they best appre-
ciated—their own.   Lavarcham could tell
the truth and so could Conachúr, but they
would not be questioned for some years to
come.

The king had downfaced the whole
matter from the start.   He went to the chase
that day.   He sat at the banquet that night.
He visited his foreign troops the next day,
and the day after he inspected the fortifications at the Pass of the Fews and a length of
the Black Pig's Dyke on either side.   There
was the Boy Troop to be reviewed and their
competitions to be scrutinized.   There were
the unending ceremonies of the court, the
Judgement Seat, and of the embassies from
all parts of his realm and from overseas:
there were gifts to be received and returned:
counsels to be given and listened to.   There
was an eternal variety of occupations for the
king, who although he might employ a day
of eighteen hours' work, could have something yet to think of ere he slept.

Cúchulinn and Conall Cearnach had been equal kings with him, but they had (Lavarcham had assisted in that) surrendered their powers to Conachúr, who was now known and described as Emperor of Ulster.

What allegiance he gave to the High King of Ireland we do not know, and it may have been part of his plan to arrive at that dignity himself. A Connacht prince was then, and for a thousand years afterwards, High King of Ireland, and although the effort of Connacht and Ulster to achieve supreme rule may now be forgotten, the effects of those bitter wars lasted longer than an historian would dare to count.

So far as Ulster was concerned the king might have been at ease. His honour was as safe as his kingdom, and as for the other actors in his drama their condition was so manifestly gentle and their youth so extreme that no taint of ugliness or treachery could remain in the tale, or in the mind of the person who heard it. It could, in a while, have been told of as a regrettable childish misadventure, and one which not even the king need further remember.

But the king remembered.

It was to escape such a memory that he plunged into affairs and banquets and a whole roystering self-expenditure which would have devitalized any other man. He prolonged his day until it could not for very weariness be further extended, and then he went to bed.

No: he went to Deirdre's bed where Naoise slept, and over which he hovered sleepless, though in sleep, and in a torment that poisoned the very sunlight when he awakened.

CHAPTER II

CONACHUR MAC NESSA was preparing a feast.

Household banquets were common matters at his court, but this was to be a State banquet, and every person who could be thought of as noble or notable was invited to the Red Branch.

As well as an aristocracy of birth there was in every Irish court an élite of excellence. Those who were foremost in learning, the arts, or the crafts, had the privilege of visiting the king equally with those whose merit rose from their fathers' graves or their skill at arms. A king was then close to his people, and he was by training and habit a connoisseur in many things which all could understand. A commonwealth of taste is the only one which can admit equality—it is democracy. He could commend with knowledge

the man who built a house or the man who
did the carvings in it. He could speak to
the maker of his chariots or the breaker of
his horses in terms that apprehended to the
last shading the matter that was being dis-
cussed, and, so, to the expert who cured his
bacon or the sturdy master who superin-
tended the brewing of his beer. All arts
were household arts; all crafts were arts;
and the knowledge of these was culture. A
gentleman would know of all the music that
was worthy of being played, for a musical
person formed part of every household. He
would remember the songs that had outlived time and could discuss their excel-
lences; and the only art which he need
regard as occult would be poetry itself; for,
while all other arts come by memory and
experiment, poetry, which is not an art,
comes solely by grace.

"Lavarcham," said Conachúr, "have you
heard any talk of the banquet?"

"Indeed, master, I have heard nothing
else."

"Will there be any notable absentees?"

"None but those who are dying of
wounds or sickness."

"Cúchulinn has stayed at home for some time now?"

"For a year after marriage one is still newly married," the Conversation-woman submitted.

"I fear that boy's love for me has bounds," Conachúr pursued.

"The king has been too kind to him," cried Lavarcham harshly.

"The king cannot help himself," he corrected, "for I love the lad, and I could no more do him an ill turn that I could do one to myself."

"I, too, love him," said Lavarcham, "but he is more forward than is proper, even in a prince."

"Can you tell me, Lavarcham, why he objected to my sovereign privilege with his wife?"

"Pride," she replied briefly. "He is prouder than ten kings."

"It is so, and it is a gentleman's prerogative to be proud," he continued. "But if such objections were allowed government would become impossible. Do the people still talk of his refusal?"

"The people know that the king did sleep with Emer."[1]

[1] Emer = pronounced Ever.

"Yes, they may know that, but do they know that Fergus slept on the other side of her as a guard?"

"No," she replied, "that is known to but five people, and they are all loyal to the king."

"Tell me," and Conachúr scrutinized her gravely, "do you love Cúchulinn better than me?"

"I love you best of all, master," said Lavarcham.

"I think you do, my friend, but they say that every woman loves the Cú."

"As to Fergus"—he muttered and went silent for a moment—"I do not yet know how much Fergus loves me. I am not sure that a loyal man would have undertaken a duty against his sovereign such as Fergus accepted for Cúchulinn."

"He did it because he loves both of you, master, and it is surely better that such an arrangement should be known only between friends."

"Possibly," said Conachúr. "And yet I had passed my word that if my right was conceded I would not touch the girl. Is a king's word not accepted any longer by

those Ferguses and Cúchulinns?" he cried
furiously.

"It was Cúchulinn's doing," said she.

"It may have been Fergus's," he retorted,
and went moodily silent. "Who knows
what that man thinks of."

"Feasts," said Lavarcham. "He loves
food."

"I was tempted," the king gritted, "to
try in the night whether he dared obstruct
me, and to see if he dared thrust the sword
he went to bed with into his king—but I had
passed my word. If," he continued irrit-
ably, "the Cú had only asked Conall Cearnach or Cruscid Menn or any gentleman
of the household to be his surety instead
of the man he did ask, I could have borne
it."

Lavarcham chuckled respectfully.

"How did that night pass, master?" she
inquired.

Conachúr gave a great laugh.

"Fergus and I went to bed, and the girl
went to bed between us, and we all had our
clothes on. My bed is small enough for
me when I am alone, but to pack a large
girl into it with all her clothes on, and then

to pack an overgrown vast bullock of a man like Fergus into it also, cannot be done. I made but one resolve that night, that on no account would I be pushed out of my own bed, and I was not, but every time that Fergus closed an eye he fell on the floor and the girl woke up and screamed."

Lavarcham let out a shrill titter, and begged the king's pardon.

"How did Emer behave?" she asked.

"She went to sleep," said Conachúr sourly. "She slept hard and kicked hard for seven long hours; and this I know, that if she has the round knee of a woman, which she has, for it was thudded into my back a thousand times, she has also the sharp elbows of a girl, so that after a time it seemed to me that there was a bundle of live bodkins in the bed. I never knew how long a night could be until that night: and we had even to prolong it out of courtesy to the lady! I shall keep a painful memory of that sweet girl until I die, and the Cú is welcome to every royal remittance he can desire on her behalf. But now, about the banquet. Is everything in order?"

"Everything, master."

"The brewers, the bakers, the cooks, they have their equipment and instructions?"

"Your butlers must answer for that, master."

"True, but as you went among these people how did they seem? What do they say about the feast?"

"They are excited and delighted. All their talk is of the famous people and the great retinues that are coming, and of how Ulster will show the Five Kingdoms what a real feast is like."

"They are good folk all," said Conachúr. "They are very good folk. You have no other news?"

"There is nothing to report, master, but that everything is well."

"You have no tidings from Scotland?"

"None, master, or little."

"Even a little news is news," said he. "Tell it, however little it be."

"They have been chased again," said Lavarcham in a low voice. "Everywhere they go they are hunted like foxes. They live under the weather, crouching like wild creatures in the bracken of a hill-side, or hiding in rocks and caves by a howling shore."

"They were delicately reared," he murmured.

"They never knew hardship," Lavarcham whimpered, "and my babe——"

"Ah yes, your babe! How old would she be now, that babe of yours?"

"Close on twenty-three years, master."

"And I am forty-seven. She has all her days in front of her still."

"What days will they be, and she quaking in a burrow like a hare, or rising thin-legged from the bog like a yellow bittern?"

"It is still the King of Scotland who pursues them?" Conachúr queried.

"Yes; since he set eyes on her seven years ago he has given them no rest, and he will give none until he has killed the three brothers and taken the girl for himself. That is the welcome of a king in Scotland. It is not the welcome the same lord got when he came here in fosterage."

"He is still a young man," said Conachúr.

"Young or old, it is not the act of a prince."

"The acts of a prince need a prince's criticism," said the king severely.

Lavarcham went silent.

"Young men go wild at times, and it is their right; but older men can be of a wildness that no young man can understand," said the king.

He twisted sternly on Lavarcham.

"Love is told of in this way and that, but it is not told of as it is. . . . It is savagery in the blood, and pain in the bone, and greed and despair in the mind. It is to be thirsty in the night and unslaked in the day. It is to carry memory like a thorn in the heart. It is to drip one's blood as one walks. Leave men to the things they know, and do you meddle with your own female businesses."

"Those children," said Lavarcham stubbornly, "are a woman's business, and his own subjects are matter for a king."

"They are our kinsmen indeed," said Conachúr thoughtfully, "and their troubles shall be looked into. We shall speak of this again after the banquet."

Lavarcham's eyes were shining.

"Yes, master," she crooned.

"Send in our butlers and all our masters," said Conachúr.

167

CHAPTER III

THE king and the guests of honour, mainly members of his family and their wives, sat on a raised dais overlooking the banqueting hall.

It was at the heart of the banquet. The food had been eaten, and mead and ale and wine were circulating. Gentlemen were politely pledging each other's ladies, and the ladies were feverishly considering each other's costumes and ornaments.

"Every one," Emer explained in her clear, sweet voice to Cúchulinn, "every one who has any hair at all wears it this way."

"It is the Connacht fashion," said Cruscraid the Stammerer.

"It is Maeve's fashion," Emer corrected.

"There must be three plaits," she continued, "two twisted round the head and

168

caught in a brooch, and one hanging down the back. I think it is a charming fashion."

"I think," Conachúr smiled, "that our ladies might content themselves with our own good Ulster customs."

"There are Ulster customs, indeed," said Emer, "but there are no fashions. One must go to Connacht for that."

"If it depended on the ladies," said Laerí, "we might let the grass grow over the Black Pig's Dyke."

"Shoulder torques are worn smaller in Connacht just now," Emer continued, eyeing superciliously the ornaments of a neighbour. "Just like mine," she added complacently.

Cúchulinn laughed boisterously.

"Just like yours," he mocked. "Why, you know well, my dove, I took that torque on the last spoil I made in Connacht."

Great good humour descended on Conachúr.

"Is that where the torque came from, my soul? Your sweet lady must show it to me more closely. You had a hard fight on that occasion?"

"I got away from them," the Cú answered modestly.

"You got away from them only when you got home," Bricriu jeered. "It was good running, my sweet."

"They were very persistent," the Cú admitted laughingly, "but I got away with my spoil."

"You know how the Connacht men explain the fact that you are still alive?"

"It will be an unpleasant explanation if it is explained by Bricriu," said Emer.

"I should like to hear it," said Conachúr.

"They are telling each other that our Cú was so beautiful they could not bear to kill him: think of that, Cúcuc."

"It is a stupid sentimental reason," growled Laerí.

"It is a good, honourable reason," Emer flashed. "It is not a reason you will ever give for letting a man escape."

"No," said Bricriu, "Laerí's excuse when he doesn't bring his man home is that he couldn't catch him."

"And that," Laerí retorted, "would be the Connacht men's reason for not getting the Cú, if a Connachtman could tell the truth about anything."

"They tell the truth when it is pleasant," said Emer, "and when it is not pleasant they tell a lie: they are a polite people, which is more than we are."

"Oh! Oh!" Conachúr laughed.

"Their lies come from a good heart and a love of happiness, while our truths come grumph, grumph, grumph like the snarling of a badly trained dog."

"Oh! Oh!" Conachúr roared.

"Conall, what do you say of these Connacht people? You also have been among them lately."

"They are honourable fighters," said Conall.

"No man can pray for a better enemy than a Connachtman," Fergus assented. "They come on where another would go back, and when they go back it is either through pity or poetry."

"Come," said Conachúr, "their compliment to the Cú has been repaid, and we can talk of something else. What do you think of our banquet?"

"There is nothing to be said," cried Emer; "it is perfect."

"Everybody seems happy," said the com-

placent king, as he looked down the Red
Branch.

His guests also stared down the hall.

"They seem happy and are happy," said
Cúchulinn. He turned to his servant and
charioteer.

"Laeg," he cried, "you do not love me!
My cup is empty."

"My darling," Laeg replied, "you have
drunk as much as is good for you."

"I shall drink as much as is bad for me if
I please," said Cúchulinn, "so bring me
some mead, my treasure."

"I shall bring you ale or cider."

"Mead," said the Cú.

"Ale, my little love," said the charioteer.

"Bring mead for the Cú when he wants
it," Emer ordered indignantly.

"Sweet mistress," said Laeg, "we have
to bring him home to-night."

"Then give him ale," said Emer.

"It will surely be ale," cried the delighted
Conachúr.

"Mead," Cúchulinn pleaded.

"You will want to fight the moon and
stars as we go home," Emer rebuked
him.

"I can fight on ale just as well," Cúchulinn asserted.

"And it is good heady ale," the king assured him.

"Let it be ale then," said Cúchulinn.

"I think that not one person whom we know is absent from this banquet," said Fiachra the Fair, Conachúr's youngest son.

The conversation turned as they all looked down the great hall. "There is So-and-so, and So-and-so."

"Who," said Emer, "is that tall, sad man with three men's chins about him?"

"He is such a one," said Fiachra.

"And the black bulk beside him with the beard that was stolen from a porcupine?"

"His name is Borach, the son of Anntè. He has a fortified rock half in and half out of the sea. He catches sharks through his window, and his banquets are all made of fish."

"He is preparing a banquet for me," Conachúr cried.

"I shall not accept a feast from that man," said Fergus.

"You must if he asks you," Cúchulinn

replied, " for it is geasa [1] on you not to refuse a feast."

"That is so, but the feast must be ready before I am offered it, and as I do not visit his part of the world I shall never have to eat his sharks."

"You think there is no one absent," asked Conachúr.

"Not one," they agreed.

"I am sharper than you all," he continued, "for I can count three who are not here."

Again they scrutinized the hall without finding any missing friends. They appealed to the herald who stood by Conachúr's chair. He, too, was mystified.

"What three are they?" said Fiachra.

"The three sons of Uisneac," the king replied smilingly. "The three Lights of Valour of the Geael."

At the words a moment's silence came on the dais and no person knew exactly what to say or do. Fergus turned his direct gaze on the king.

"They are in Scotland," he said.

"They went there seven years ago when Naoise ran away with Deirdre," said Conachúr.

---

[1] geasa=taboo.

174

Conall Cearnach turned his harsh forehead to the king.

"They are in great distress," he said.

"I have just heard so," the king replied gravely. "We must bring them home."

At the words the face of every person changed. It was as though a cordial had been dropped into each heart.

Cúchulinn flashed enthusiasm and delight at the king:

"You will let them come back?"

"They shall be at our next banquet."

"If I could love you more," Fergus affirmed, "I would love you more for that."

"I know you love me well," said Conachúr, "and I love you, my heart."

"We have been wearying to see Naoise again," cried Cúchulinn.

"What is he like?" said Emer.

"He is under geasa about his return," Bricriu interposed.

Conachúr turned abruptly to him.

"What geasa is that?"

"He will come back in the company of Fergus or of Conall or of the Cú, otherwise he will not come back."

"Ah!" said Conachúr.

175

"He was always a sensible, far-seeing boy," Bricriu continued thoughtfully.

The king's eye rested on Bricriu for one weighty moment ere he replied:

"We shall send one of the three, or all of the three to fetch him."

"What is she like?" Emer insisted.

Bricriu replied:

"She has been sleeping in ditches for six years. She will be like nothing that you have ever heard of, sweet lady."

"She——" said Cúchulinn.

"She——" said every voice at the one moment.

"She," said Conachúr with a grave smile, "was called the Troubler; she has given and received her share of trouble."

CHAPTER IV

"You understand?" said the king.

"I understand well, master," said Lavar-cham.

"First you are to send Conall to me. Half an hour afterwards you shall send Cúchulinn. In another half-hour you shall send me Fergus, and when he comes you shall see that Borach is in waiting."

"I understand well, master."

"In a little while you shall see your babe again."

She scrutinized his face humbly and gravely.

"You are most gentle, master."

"Are you not contented?"

"I am filled with joy and grief," she answered.

"And grief!" the king echoed mildly.

"She will not be the girl I knew," said Lavarcham.

"How so?"

"She will have been destroyed by hardship."

"Girls are tougher than women pretend," said Conachúr.

"A man grows directly from the boy he was," she continued. "He keeps the boy you knew even when he is an old man. But a girl grows suddenly at an angle to all that she was. She becomes a stranger in a year."

"Hum!" he scoffed.

"The Deirdre we knew is dead, and some weather-wise, weather-wasted woman will look at me with unknown eyes and say, 'How do you do.' I shall not know how to talk to her," said Lavarcham.

"If it is so we shall see it so," said Conachúr. "Go now and send me Conall, and then the others in the order I told you."

Lavarcham left the room.

When she was beyond the king's hearing she stood for a good five minutes musing deeply within herself; listening as it were to her heart, to her instincts, to that monitor on whom we call when the times are moment-

ous and doubtful and there is no other help
but our own to be summoned. She sighed
inaudibly, tremulously, and went about her
business.

Conall Cearnach stood in the doorway.

"Good, O Chief and King!" he saluted.

"Life and happiness!" Conachúr replied
briskly. "Sit here, my heart, for there is
but one chair. I shall walk up and down
while we discuss this business."

His guest sat down.

"It is about Uisneac's boys. You think
they should come home?"

"Every one thinks so; there is a gap
among your gentlemen while they are away."

Conachúr nodded.

"There is an even worse gap among your
captains."

"It is so."

"And among the boys growing from the
troop," Conall resumed, "there is no one to
replace these three. They were already at
the force of manhood, and even then their
skill and knowledge was remarkable."

"True," Conachúr agreed. "They were
trained by me."

"The last six years of combat and ambuscade and flight will have made them but the better soldiers."

The king strode to his visitor and laid a hand on his shoulder.

"Conall, my friend, these three have treated me shamefully."

"The only way to forgive a thing is to forget it. You have forgiven, Conachúr—and forgotten."

"If they returned with you, Conall, and if evil happened to them while under your surety, what would you do?"

Conall rose from his chair, and in rising displaced the king's hand. He looked at the king with his steady, pale regard.

"If evil came to a person placed under my protection I would kill the person by whom that evil came."

Conachúr laughed merrily.

"Even the king himself?" he quizzed.

"I would kill any person that dishonoured me," said Conall sternly.

"You would be quite right to do so," said Conachúr heartily.

He seated himself in the chair that Conall had vacated.

"The matter I wish to discuss is your uncle, Cet mac Magach, Cet of Connacht. That man scorns our borders, and his depredations are costly and impertinent. Our young men also are not equal to that able reiver. Could you not talk to him, Conall, and draw him off us?"

"I talk to Connachtmen with a sword."

"You may talk to him that way if you please."

Conall reviewed the invitation imperturbably.

"I would not care to kill Cet mac Magach. He is my mother's brother."

"And he is not an easy person to kill," said Conachúr. "We shall make our own arrangements about him. Blessings and long life to you!"

The dismissed champion strode from the room.

"That man," Conachúr thought moodily, "has been hammered together stone by stone, and is no more than a petrified vanity. He loves nothing but his honour, which is that he loves himself."

"Come in, the Cú," he called. "Come in, and an hundred welcomes, my sweet lad."

181

Cúchulinn, magnificent in red silk and gold embroideries, came leaping in.

"Well, my pulse!" cried Conachúr. "And you have a new mantle!"

"Emer made it," the Cú boasted. "She does the finest embroidery in the world. She told me so herself."

"If she told you so——" said Conachúr. "Let me look at the sleeve. It is not bad, my delight. But I have a few pieces somewhere—Did you pass Conall Cearnach as you came in?"

"I did; he smiled a frozen smile at me, and clapped my shoulder with a fist of lead."

"We were arguing about honour. If a person was placed under your protection and was then killed, what would you do, Cúcuceen?"

"I would kill the other person," said Cúchulinn.

"If it was the king, my pet?"

"I would kill the king."

Conachúr sat round at him in a rage.

"Would you kill me?" he demanded.

"I would," Cúchulinn returned as fiercely. "I would kill any one who destroyed a person under my protection."

"You would *not* kill me, Cúchulinn!"

"As sure as dawn begins the day."

"Begone, young puppy.   Begone, cockscomb," he thundered.

"Honour———" Cúchulinn commenced.

"You do not love me," the king stormed.

"I do love you."

"Begone," the king roared, and stamped the floor.

The laughing Cúchulinn backed before his rage.

"I do love you," he shouted; and he continued to shout, "I love you . . . I love you," until he reached the end of the corridor and turned the corner, where the guards poked each other in the ribs and giggled with joy.

Conachúr tugged at his beard half in anger and half in laughter.

Another vanity in a mantle, he thought. That boy loves me indeed, and he would as surely kill me, for it is certain that I could not think of killing him.   Is there no person in my realm who loves me better than his own poor pride?   And what a three that— Naoise—must choose for his sureties!

He strode savagely up and down the room.

183

"We shall see now what Fergus is like," he sneered. "He professes to adore me, and eyes me with the devotion of a dull dog. A dull dog he is, and a monster of sufficiency to boot."

If he dares to thwart me—the king gloomed, and went into a bitter rage of meditation.

A great voice boomed on him.

"Good, my soul, Conachúr!"

"It is Fergus," cried the king joyfully, and strode to meet his visitor.

"Come, my pulse and best. Sit you and I shall stand. Nay, sit," he chided gently. "Indeed, if things were right you should sit always, and this man," tapping his own breast, "should bend a lover's knee before you. You bear no ill-will, sweetheart, for that trick of long ago?"

The giant sat.

"I never think of it, or I think of it with relief when I remember the Judgement Seat, and the knots and tangles and questions that came day by day. I was not bad at justice, but I was a sad fumbler at law, and the best man has the best place, my dear. Do not torment yourself with memories of that old——"

He halted for a word.

"Treachery," said Conachúr.

"That is not the word I wanted," Fergus laughed. "You are too sensitive, Conachúr. The nobles agreed and I agreed that you should be the king, and I am your most loving subject."

"You do love me?"

"Have I not proved it?" the other smiled.

"Many a time. Times out of mind," said Conachúr.

He turned aside and closed his eyes. A pang of dull hate smouldered and stirred in him.

"If this man were dead," he thought with weary despair. "If this man would but cease and disappear and begone, how free my soul could be."

He turned again to Fergus.

"Let us talk of other things," he said. "Those sons of Uisneac——"

"You did a rare deed there," said the other approvingly.

"Rare or not rare they will be brought back and you shall go for them."

Fergus nodded.

185

"If they claim my protection——" he began.

"They do claim it, and they will return under your protection."

"Then I shall go for them. I shall be glad to see these boys again: they had the makings of great fighters in them."

"That is settled," said Conachúr. "You can start to-day?" he inquired.

"I can start within the hour."

"Good."

Conachúr mused, and turned thoughtful eyes on his companion.

"If anything happened to these three while they were under your protection, Fergus, what would you do?"

"I would kill the person who interfered with my protection."

"No matter who it was?"

"No matter who it was."

"I wonder would our mutual love withstand even an attack on honour," said Conachúr thoughtfully. "There are bounds to love, but I doubt that I could lift a hand against you even if you attacked my honour."

"Our love is a great bond," said Fergus simply; "it would be hard to destroy."

"Nevertheless," the king smiled, "if I injured your honour; say that I attacked these sons of Uisneac while in your surety, your affection for me would scarcely withstand that."

"That would be a hard case indeed," Fergus laughed.

"You would kill me?" the king queried with a genial smile.

"You know," said Fergus, "that I could not kill you whatever you did."

"We love one another well," said Conachúr. "It is a great thing to love as we do, my friend."

"But now," he continued briskly, "we must attend to this troublesome business, and we must have a third person present in order that the world may know how we despatch it."

He clapped his hands, and, to the servant who appeared:

"Who is in waiting?"

"Borach, lord."

"Tell him to come here."

"That is the man who feeds his guests on sharks," said Fergus.

"He is on duty of honour to-day," the

king replied carelessly, "and he will be
witness to the world of my instructions
and of your charge. Come forward, good
Borach."

The bulky man strode in.

"You shall listen to my instructions to our
dear Fergus and you shall be the witness to
this arrangement."

Fergus thereupon stood up and Conachúr
seated himself.

"Fergus, my friend, you shall go to
Scotland and bring back to this court the
three sons of Uisneac and the woman
Deirdre. There shall be no delay about
the execution of this duty."

"There shall be no delay," Fergus
affirmed.

"The instant they set foot in Ireland you
shall proceed here with them; and if, from
any cause whatsoever, you cannot come
yourself, you shall cause them to come to
me without the delay of even one half-
hour."

"That will be done," said Fergus, "but
I shall be with them."

"With you or without you, whether they
arrive by day or by night in Ireland, they

shall be sent here to me without the delay of even one half-hour."

"That will be done," said Fergus.

"I bind that on you to the letter," said Conachúr.

"I accept it so," Fergus returned. "I shall bring my two sons to Scotland, and if, by any miracle, I should be delayed myself, they shall go forward with every speed and deliver these four people safely at Emain Macha."

"A speedy return to you," said Conachúr. "Go at once, my dear friend. But you, Borach, stay yet awhile. I have the matter of our feast to discuss with you."

Fergus smiled broadly as he withdrew.

"Sharks," he murmured quite joyfully. "Sharks!"

CHAPTER V

ON the slope of a sunny hill overlooking Loch Eitche, Deirdre was cooking the meal which her husband and his brothers had run to earth and carried home on their shoulders.

"The food is ready," she called.

"It is not as ready as I am, for I could eat land and water," Ardan averred.

"We shall not give you any," she mocked.

"Serve the greedy person right," said Ainnle. "He eats in his sleep."

"But I must get the part I killed," Ardan protested.

"What part is that?"

"I don't know its name, but it is the tenderest part."

"This is also a thievish person," said

Ainnle indignantly; "he is trying to claim the part I killed."

"Fight for me, Naoise!" Ardan implored. "Be on my side, Deirdreen!"

"You shall be served last," said Deirdre severely, "and you shall get a tough piece."

"Ochone! ochone for ever!" he lamented.

"How do you like that piece?" said Deirdre vindictively.

"I could eat a cow's horn if you cooked it," he wheedled. "Won't you give me more in a minute, little sister?"

"I shall give you ten kisses," said Deirdre.

"Do not go between that man and his meat," Ainnle warned; "he will bite you."

"The law says that you are my brother, but I shall certainly divorce you," the other cried, "and then you will be sorry."

"You are silent, Naoise!" said Deirdre.

"No man can talk with his mouth full except me," Ardan explained.

"Half an hour ago," said Naoise, "I saw a ship beating in from the sea."

"A fishing-boat?"

"I think it was a boat from Ireland."

"Why should you think so?"

"It had the cut of an Irish boat."

"If it is any of our friends from Ireland," said Ainnle, "they will be almost at the strand now."

"We have no friends in Ireland," Deirdre returned coldly.

"Run to the strand, Ardan my pulse, and see who came in that ship."

The boy scrambled to his feet.

"If they are friends I'll give them kisses. If they are enemies I'll steal their supper."

But Deirdre was woe-begone as she looked on the two brothers.

"What ails you, little sister?" Ainnle inquired.

"I had a dream last night," she replied, "and it troubles me."

"We share all things, and our troubles. Tell us your dream."

Deirdre looked away distantly to the sea.

"I dreamed that three birds came flying from Emain Macha."

"Happy birds," said Naoise dreamily, "that can fly, and fly back."

"They had each a sip of honey in their beaks. They left the three sips of honey

with us, and they took away from us three
sips of our blood."

"The ending," said Naoise, "is not so
sweet as the beginning."

"How do you interpret that dream?" his
brother asked.

"I think that three people will come to
us carrying a sweet, deceitful message from
Conachúr."

"A dream is a dream," he soothed her.

"And my dreams!" she cried. "How
many times have we fled on the advice of
my dream? and as we looked back we
saw that happening which we fled from. Is
that true, brother?"

"It is true. Our Deirdre has second
sight."

Naoise turned his shoulder along the
grass, and laid his ear to the wind.

"I hear a shout," he said.

"It is some man of these parts giving a
hunting call," she answered.

"It seemed to me like the shout of an
Irishman."

"It may be Ardan returning."

"It is not his call."

"It is Fergus and his two sons," said

Deirdre miserably. "They are coming to us with three sips of honey in their mouths."

"What is in Fergus's mouth is in his heart also," Naoise cried joyfully. "One time or another even your dream may be wrong, for if Fergus agrees to be a messenger the message will be as true as his own truth."

"Remember," said Deirdre, "that I told you they were coming without having seen them."

Fergus and his two sons, with Ardan doing circles and whoops around them, rose on a slope of the hill, and came striding over the tussochs. Behind them came the shield-bearer and the shield itself, and at the sight Ainnle fled to meet them, but Naoise drew back to keep Deirdre company, for she had not moved.

"It is Fergus," he said, with shining eyes.

"He has come for our blood," said white-lipped Deirdre.

"Queen of queens," her husband laughed, "you do not know Fergus."

At that the whole band came together, and they all kissed each other fondly.

"Welcome to this land," said Naoise.

"And thou art Deirdre!" cried Fergus, as he kissed her on either cheek.

She smiled wanly as she returned his kisses.

"We shall teach you to laugh in Ireland," he trolled.

"What news is there from the lovely country?" her husband demanded.

"The best. The news that you are to return there."

"Ah!" said Naoise.

"The king himself has sent me to bring you home under my surety and protection."

"Whoo-oop!" said Ardan.

"He bids me tell you that he has forgiven you and wishes you all happiness."

But Deirdre turned to him, smiling and fearful.

"We are happy here in Scotland," she said.

"Nay," said Fergus, "one cannot be satisfied when one is in exile, for his native land is dearer to a man than any other."

"This is truly a dear country," she replied.

"And it is well known," Fergus continued, "that if a man of Ireland had the lordship of another country he would yet be unhappy unless he could see Ireland every day."

"It is so," said Ainnle.

"There is no one knows its truth better than the sons of Uisneac," cried Naoise.

"You see," the great man chided her.

"I know that this is a dear land," said Deirdre stubbornly, "and that here the sons of Uisneac might rise to any destiny they aimed for."

"It may be so," Naoise affirmed. "But Ireland is dearer to me than Scotland."

"Scotland is safer," she said.

"Will you be safer in Scotland than with me?" cried Fergus in amazement. "I have yet a little power," he smiled.

"We will go with you," said Naoise.

"Do not go, my pulse," said Deirdre in great agitation. "Do not trust yourself where Conachúr is."

"Women and cats dislike change," Naoise laughed, "but you will love this change."

In half an hour they strode down the hill,

and in an hour their sails were bent for Ireland.

It was then Deirdre made her first poem, beginning

> A lovable land is that in the east,
> Marvellous Alba . . .

CHAPTER VI

As they approached harbour they noticed a band waiting at the landing-place, and these people raised mighty cheers as the ship swung.

"That man!" said Fergus, indicating one who stood apart and issued commands. "I surely know that man! It is Borach," he laughed. "It is the man who feeds people on sharks," and he explained to his party all that he had heard of Borach at the banquet.

"The gods be praised," he murmured, "we cannot wait for his feast even if he offers it."

When they landed Borach ran to meet them. He kissed Fergus three times, and he kissed each of the others also.

"Welcome to this land," he said; "all Ireland welcomes you."

He looked with his black, deep-set peep
at Deirdre and kissed her, but when she
looked at him he turned aside.

He was ill at ease, and all his move-
ments were self-conscious and unhappy. He
turned, almost truculently, to Fergus.

"Fergus," he said, "I am honoured to
see you in my lordship."

"You are kind," said Fergus, "and I
shall bind you to visit me in mine."

"I am so delighted," Borach continued
hastily, "that I have prepared a feast for you,
such as is only offered to a king."

"The king did say," Fergus rumbled
joyfully, "that you had a feast ready for
him."

"That is the feast I am offering to you,"
said Borach.

"What?" cried the giant.

"The king has notified me that he cannot
come to my banquet, so I am offering it to
you instead."

Fergus stared at him:

"You were present, and you heard
Conachúr's instructions that there should be
no delay on this journey. I shall come and
feast with you another time, my dear."

"I insist that you stay and feast with me for one week," Borach growled.

"You insist!" he murmured in astonishment.

"I invoke your geasa," said the other stubbornly. "You must remain with me for a week."

At that Fergus became one purple mass from the crown of his head to the soles of his feet, and his face swelled so that the bystanders feared he would burst with the excess and violence of his rage. Borach was nervous, but his own men were around him, and although he was terrified of Fergus he was yet more frightened of the king.

"I insist," he shouted, "and you cannot refuse a feast that is offered to you kindly."

"This is a trick," said Fergus. "You know my oath; you listened to it, for the king made me swear in your very presence, that, was it by day or by night, I should speed the sons of Uisneac to him from the moment we landed. And you offer me a feast and a week's delay! What dog's deed do you intend, you Borach? Do you not value your life?" he roared.

"I value my life indeed," Borach replied, "and," looking round on his attendants, "and I shall take great care of it. I hold you to the feast, Fergus."

"Come apart with me," said the bewildered giant to his companions, "and let us discuss this wonder."

"What ought we to do?" he asked.

"It seems that you must make a choice," said Deirdre timidly.

"What choice is there, sweet queen?"

"You have to choose whether you will forsake the feast or forsake us," she murmured.

Her heart swelled as she spoke, so that her voice was not steady, for she was astonished and unhappy and her mind was bewildered.

"In truth I must leave one or the other," said Fergus.

Naoise and his brothers stared at the fogged noble.

"Dear champion," she pleaded, "it would be more fitting to leave the feast, but it would not be right to leave us in the middle of our enemies."

"But I cannot leave a feast," Fergus

explained, "for that is my compact with the gods. One cannot break his geasa."

They stared at him and at one another in consternation.

"Whatever is in his mind, this Borach will not release me from the eating of his accursed sharks," Fergus continued wrathfully. "Eat them I must, but I shall leave my sons with you, and they will protect you on the road to Emain."

"By my hand," said Naoise, "you are doing a great deal for us! The protection we seek is that of your name and fame and station. Any other protection we do not value, for we are well used to taking care of ourselves."

"But——" said Fergus.

"We did not come here under your weapons," said Naoise, "we came under your guarantee."

"You mistake me," said Fergus mildly. "My sons carry my guarantee, and with them you will be as secure as though I were present."

He turned to Rough-Red Buinne and Iollann the Fair.

"Is not that so?"

"It is so," said Buinne.

"The Council of All Ireland would not tolerate the breaking of this notable surety," said Iollann. "It is known now through the whole country."

"And what man would dare to break my guarantee?" Fergus inquired.

Naoise bit his lip.

"Let us go on," said he.

He turned his level gaze on Fergus' sons.

"You are our guarantors," he said, "and we accept your protection."

They returned to where the black-avised chieftain was waiting, and him Fergus stared and out-stared until he was reduced to a mass of unhappiness.

"I shall eat sharks because I must, Borach," he thundered.

"What sharks are you talking about?" said Borach.

"Lead me to your miseries of the deep," said Fergus, "but do not talk to me about them."

CHAPTER VII

As the travellers proceeded they were morose and thoughtful, and even Ardan's high spirits flagged. But as they looked on a native sky and on the fields and hedge-rows of an Irish countryside something of their disquietude was eased and a lightening of the heart became apparent in each of them.

"Dear girl," said Naoise, and he placed an arm about her shoulders. "We are in Ireland," he said.

At the word every misery fled from Ardan's breast, so that he began to look truculently on his brother Ainnle, and even to give him an occasional shoulder as they marched.

Deirdre leaned to her husband.

"I have had other visions," she said.

She moved her hand languidly towards Fergus' two sons, who strode a few paces in advance.

"These are our sureties!" she mocked.

"They represent their father," Naoise affirmed.

"They represent nothing but themselves," she answered, "and if their father leaves us for a feast, they will leave us for any other prank."

"It was his geasa," said Naoise patiently.

"Whatever it was," said Deirdre.

"We are utterly alone," she continued. "We have no backing of any kind, and we will arrive in Emain Macha at the absolute mercy of Conachúr."

She seized her husband's arm.

"You also are under geasa not to return unless in the company of Fergus. He may be delayed for a week. Let us camp here and wait until he comes up with us."

"Dear child," said Naoise, "how can we insult these good youths?"

But Deirdre was in terrible agitation.

"I dread appearing in the presence of Conachúr if Fergus is not by us."

"His guarantee is with us," and Naoise

205

indicated the two young men—"There it is, four legs of it marching stoutly."

"At least," she pleaded, "let us go to Cúchulinn's fortress in Dun Dealgan and wait there until he or Fergus can come with us—if you will do that, I shall complain no more."

"Fergus," he replied, "has bound himself before the king that he would send us on without an hour's delay."

"And he bound himself to stay with us, but he has broken his word."

"We must keep his word for him with the king," said Naoise.

"Another person's honour is another person's business. That compact is broken by him, and your geasa is not kept by keeping his. Let us turn to Dun Dealgan and take Cúchulinn's protection."

Naoise indicated the two who were marching in front.

"I shall ask their advice, and if they agree to it we will go to Dun Dealgan."

He called the two, and put the question to them. But they were scandalized.

"You have no confidence in us," said Buinne.

"And none in our father's word," said Iollann.

"This woe has come on us because of your father's word, and he has left us in our danger for a feast," she raged.

"The whole world," said Buinne, "knows Fergus mac Roy, and the worth of his protection—You know it," he said to Naoise, "although your queen does not."

"You are right," said Naoise. "We may go on without misgiving, my dove."

And they went on.

On their journey the next day they reached Slieve Fuad. Deirdre strayed behind and in the movement and conversation her absence was not noticed for a long time. Naoise retraced his path from the White Cairn of the Watching, and came on her sleeping in a grassy hollow. When he awakened her she stared and clutched him, and cried wildly and bitterly.

"What is it?" he asked in alarm.

"I have had a vision," she sobbed. "I have had a dreadful vision."

"What did you see?"

"I saw Iollann with no head on him and

I saw Buinne with his head safe on his shoulders."

Naoise took her in his arms.

"Be glad," he laughed, "that one of our friends will escape the doom you have planned for us all."

But she stared at him in distraction.

"No friend of ours will escape," she moaned.

"But Buinne kept his head on in your dream!"

"The man who had no head had been fighting for us, and the man who had a head was fighting against us," she whispered.

Naoise was shocked.

"How you have changed, my one treasure," he said mournfully.

She threw her arms about him.

"Do not speak unkindly to me," she begged.

"That lovely mouth spoke always lovely things, and now it speaks nothing but evil."

She closed his lips with her hand.

"No, no," she said. "Do not say more. Or say only that you love me. You do love me, my husband?"

"Little tender wife!" he smiled. "After all the dangers we have gone through you are frightened at last."

"Yes," she breathed, "I am terribly frightened. I die of fear for us all. When I remember Conachúr . . . He looked so at me, Naoise! He——! Come with me to Scotland. We will be safe there. We will be happy again. We will hunt in the Woods of Cuan and Glen da Rua. I shall never complain again in this life if you will come with me to Scotland. Let us go away. You and I, and our darlings, Ainnle and Ardan. He is so young to be killed, our brother Ardan. He is but twenty-one years old, and he is gay and loving and fearless. We will be together again; we four: alone and happy. Listen! we will hunt and feast and defend ourselves and fear nothing. You shall win a kingdom there: in sweet Alba of the heathery uplands; but let us fly from Conachúr. You do not know him. Only I and Lavarcham know that terrible king. He is thoughtful. He is bitter and unforgiving, and his memories are rooted deep like the roots of a deep tree."

But Naoise put her hands away.

"If you must speak badly of others," he said coldly, "speak to me of foreigners, and not of my own people!"

"Alas, my husband!" said Deirdre. "Alas and alas for all of us!"

She rose wearily.

"Do not be angry with me. Let that last unhappiness be spared me. I am your wife, Naoise. I would prefer that evil should happen to all the world rather than one small misfortune should come to you. I am not Deirdre any more. I am Misery."

But he kissed and petted her, putting back the hair from her brow and framing her face in his hands.

"We are here now," he said, "and no matter what awaits us we must go to meet it. You would not wish me to run away, Deirdreen."

"We ran away before," she said, "and we have greater reason to run away now than we had then. The spider is waiting for us in the web."

"You forget, and you will keep on forgetting it, that we are under the protection of Fergus, and through him we are under the protection of all Ireland."

But she looked at him almost angrily.

"Fergus," she scoffed. "He is a traitor that Fergus. He is being used by the king to betray us."

Naoise bit his lip and his eyes became hard and sombre.

"Let us go on," he said. "We should reach Ard Saileach ere the evening."

CHAPTER VIII

THEY stood on the slope of a hill in a rounded and rolling country looking down on Emain Macha. The evening was advanced, and the late sunlight, all a glimmer of gold, was shining tenderly on the city, so that the mighty, ten-acre palace of Conachúr shone back again as though it also were a sun. The great bronze doors, polished like mirrors, were blazing in red lakes of flame, the glass windows of the women's sunny rooms were like blinding pools of gold, and the roofs, painted in broad reaches of red and green and orange, glowed and sparkled in the mellow evening.

"It is good to look on that again," said Naoise in a low voice.

"I had almost forgotten it," said Ainnle.

But Ardan squatted in the grass and stared and stared with his soul in his eyes.

"You have not seen the city for seven years!" said Buinne.

Naoise drew Deirdre to him.

"Are you not contented now, my heart?"

"Our wanderings are ended," he continued tenderly. "We are outlaws no more, and that long vagabondage is done with. You will sleep at last in a bed," he smiled.

"Oh, my dear!" she breathed.

"We are home again," he said, and his heart filled suddenly so that he could not tell if it were really joy that stayed his tongue and blinded his eyes, or if the grief of seven long years had risen within him like a wintry tide.

But Deirdre was not happy. She saw Ainnle's contained joy, and the ecstacy in Ardan's eyes.

"Alas, my darlings!" she said.

"You still think," said Naoise, "that the king of such a land can act towards us like a traitor?"

"I shall give you a sign," she replied mournfully and gently. "If Conachúr lodges us this night in his own house we are safe."

"He has sent for us of his own royal will," said Ainnle, "and he will lodge us as is proper, in the Royal Branch."

"Poor trusting gentlemen!" said Deirdre. "Conachúr could not live again in the house where you three had lodged. He will send us to the Red Branch."

"And if he does?" said Naoise.

"I," Ardan cried, "am going to put a new edge on my sword if he does. There is a good edge on it already," he explained, "but I am going to put edges all over it."

"If we are sent to the Red Branch," said Ainnle, "I shall let you give my blade a rub too."

"I call on Iollann and Buinne for protection," Ardan cried indignantly. "That man makes me work for him like a horse," he complained.

Naoise turned to the two sons of Fergus.

"If we are sent to the Red Branch what will you do?"

"We will go there with you," said Buinne.

"The king's house is always filled with guests," Iollann said. "He cannot know just when we should arrive, and he may have no place for us at a moment's notice."

214

"There is nothing Conachúr does not know," said Deirdre. "Borach will have sent a runner to tell of our arrival, and his own spies will have told the king in what place we camped each night, and at what hour we marched again in the morning. He knows now that we are here, and if he sends us to the Red Branch we are lost."

"I am as full of curiosity as an old woman," Naoise laughed. "Let us go on and find out everything that is going to happen."

In a short time they were among the streets and booths around Emain Macha, but the twilight had descended and the passers-by did not recognize the six travellers.

"Yonder is the Speckled Branch, the Armoury," said Ainnle. "The Boy Troop will be going to bed shortly. You remember those nights, Naoise, and all the chattering?"

"And the climbing out of windows by a cord," said Ardan. "And the scrambling back again while the comrades above threw all the world at the guards who were trying to stick spears in us as we shinned up."

"There is the Red Branch," said Naoise.

"Is it truly full of dead men's heads?"
Deirdre chattered through frozen lips.

"There is generally a head or two," he
answered carelessly, "Connachtmen mostly."

"Very hairy, beardy, toothy kinds of
heads," said Ardan. "I remember them,
and they used to get hairier and beardier
and toothier every second day. At last,"
he explained to Deirdre, "there wouldn't
be any head at all, no face at all, only a mat
of hair as long as a woman's, and it in knots,
and a shiny grin among the knots."

"You are all wrong," said Ainnle. "A
dead man's hair grows lank and long like
a drink of water."

"Pooh!" said Ardan. "You remember
everything! You are the great man of the
world! The wind knots them and twists
them and wobbles them all in and out like
a doormat."

"Yonder is Conachúr's house, the Royal
Branch," said Naoise.

"We will give a good thundering knock
at the door and make them jump," said
Ainnle gleefully.

"I'll give it a kick," said Ardan.

Naoise did give a thundering knock.

The door opened and a guard appeared.

"Who asks admission at this hour?" he demanded.

"The sons of Uisneac."

The guard stared.

"Come in, nobles, and sit for a moment while I seek instructions."

"Let a message be sent to the king," said Buinne, "that the protection of Fergus mac Roy and those he protects have arrived as he ordered."

The chamberlain came, Scel, son of Barnene.

"The household have retired," he said. "But the king sends his regrets and courtesies, and has instructed that his noble guests are to be lodged in the Red Branch for this night. A guard will escort you there." He motioned to the captain of the guard, who ranged his men.

"Don't forget about the edges you promised to do for me," said Ardan to his brother.

"No wriggling, young lazy-bones," Ainnle retorted. "You shall do your work and be respectful to your betters also."

"Is not that man a tyrant?" said Ardan.

He turned to the captain of the guard. "Hold me away from him, good sir," he implored.

"I am at your orders, gentlemen," said the smiling captain.

CHAPTER IX

BUT Conachúr had not retired.

He was seated in the central room away in the heart of his monstrous palace, and the great crystal ball swung at his shoulder. He had stared into it for hours and had seen nothing.

Lavarcham also was there, seated humbly on a stool.

"Fill my cup," said Conachúr. "I am thirsty to-night, my heart. I could drain a sea and not drown this thirst."

"You are troubled, lord. All this business has fevered you."

"And you! Are you not excited at the thought of seeing your babe again?"

"I have interested myself in so many things these seven long years, master, I have almost forgotten her. She has dropped out

219

of my mind, and now I would as readily not
see her as see her."

"I thought you loved that babe!"

"After all, she is not my babe. Felimid
mac Dall's wife bore her."

"Is it so?" Conachúr mused. "I had
almost forgotten that old tale."

"I had but the labour of rearing her, and
of being disappointed by her," she said
bitterly.

"You did not fill my cup, Lavarcham."

"I did, master, but you have emptied it."

"Fill it again, good friend. . . . She was
beautiful, Lavarcham! She was a thing of
joy and wonder!"

"Young girls are beautiful while they are
young, master, but in a few years they look
like any other person."

"You think so?"

"They get fat or they get thin. It is not
girls that are lovely, master, it is youth."

"And I am forty - seven years of age!
The years go by doing what I know to me,
but for her there has been only the time to
ripen what was immature. The green fruit
will be ruddy and fragrant worked on by the

sun and the wind.   What age is she now,
woman?"

"She is seven years older in time, and
twenty years older in hardship.   She will
have forgotten how to lie in a bed, or how to
eat proper food."

"She will surely have changed," said
Conachúr.

A brisk moment returned to the great
man, and he aroused himself.

"How will she look after her years of
lying in the butt of a wet ditch or in the bog?"

"Ah me!" said Lavarcham.

"She will have plodded over tough hills
with a thin belly and a dry lip.   She will
have slept with her fingers in her mouth to
keep them warm in the winter.   She will
be lean and red-handed and windy-faced;
with the arches of her feet broken down by
too much walking, and her knees sagging
under her like an old ploughman's.   Is that
how the Troubler will look, Lavarcham?"

"I think, master, that she may be a long,
thin, tough woman.   She will be rheu-
matic——"

"She will awaken in the night coughing
like a sick horse," said the cheerful king.

"I do not wish to see her," said Lavar-cham sourly.

"No more do I," said Conachúr. "Let her go. . . . My cup!" he murmured. "Lavarcham, you do not attend me well."

Again he became moody.

"If I were not the king I would steal to the Red Branch and spy on her ruin through a window. I should like to see that she is lank and depressed. . . . Go you, Lavar-cham; the guards know your privileges. Look through the window and bring me back that tale."

"I do not want to see her at all, master. Let her stay with the people she has chosen, and let her torment our sleep no more."

"Go, nevertheless, and bring me a full account of her. Fill up my glass. Ex-amine her carefully, my soul, so that you can bring me a true report. But do not delay, for I shall be waiting for you. I am lonely to-night, woman; I am very lonely. Send me a man of the guard to fill my cup!"

Lavarcham, with every sign of distaste, almost of annoyance, set on her errand.

"Sit there, and take your ease," the king

ordered the guard who came in. "Do not stare at the floor, good soul, nor at the ceiling. Ah me! stand behind my chair then, and when my cup is empty refill it for me."

The embarrassed soldier moved gratefully to cover, and the king fell again to his woeful meditations.

"Guard!" he said.

"A Rí Uasal!" the guard rolled sonorously.

"Have you ever looked in a crystal?"

"Never, king."

"Look in this crystal, my friend. Can you see anything?"

"There is a fog in the crystal."

"It has been there these three days. Look again, good lad."

"I think there is a woman's face."

"What sort of a woman?"

"It has gone, majesty."

"What sort was she?"

"I saw the loveliest face that ever brightened the world. It seemed like the face of a sky-woman or a lady of the Shí."

"Sit on this little stool, and fill my cup."

"What age are you, guard?"

"Twenty-two years, majesty."

"What is your name?"

"I am called Strong Fist, sir."

"I remember you, Tréndorn, you are my hereditary man. Your father was my man before you. How did he die?"

"He was killed by Naoise, the son of Uisneac, sir."

"I remember," said Conachúr, "and your two brothers were killed by that Naoise. Do you remember that also?"

"I would not forget it, sir."

"There are things that one should not forget, guard. Would you do an ill turn to the same Naoise?"

"If I had that chance I would take it, sir."

"He is in the Red Branch," said Conachúr. "He is there with the woman whose face you saw in the crystal. Go there for me, good soldier, and look through the window. See that no person within observes you, for these are murderous and skilful men, and if they saw you they would stop your breath."

The guard stood glowering.

"In what way do I get equal with Naoise?" he demanded.

"Each thing in its time, good soul, for

you would not understand how the king moves. This is but the first step, and the second shall be taken in no short time. Climb to the window, and look carefully at the woman who is there with Naoise. Examine her well and bring me back news of how she seems and what she looks like. You have seen women before?"

"I have, majesty."

"You know what to look for; you will know how to look at a woman. Go. Fill my cup, guard, and go on my errand."

CHAPTER X

"STILL," said Ardan, "we are not treated too badly. There is plenty of food."

"And there are beds in the alcove," said Ainnle.

"We shall sleep well to-night," said Deirdre, and she burst into tears.

They sat dumb, each feeling as if a chill wind had touched him.

"Forgive me," said Deirdre. "I shall not complain any more. Let us sit to our meat."

"I shall eat and eat and eat," said Ardan. "I am so hungry I could growl over my food."

"You shall be served first, Ardaneen," said Deirdre, "and if there is one tender piece you shall have it."

"Our Buinne is even hungrier than I am, let him have the first piece."

Deirdre looked kindly at Buinne, but as she looked her eyes widened and she went white to the lips. She spoke to him with a shy smile.

"You will have the first piece, Buinne," she stammered.

"I shall take what comes," said Rough-Red Buinne.

Deirdre sank back in her chair.

"Naoise, my dear," she said, "please carve for me. I am not well."

"Buinne is sensible," said Naoise. "He has a head on his shoulders." He stumbled in his carving, and cast a swift glance at Deirdre.

"The first portion," he continued gravely, "shall be for Buinne, the second for Iollann, the third for Deirdre, the fourth for Ainnle, the fifth for Ardan, and the sixth for Naoise."

"My piece is to be the tenderest," said Ardan complacently, "Deirdre said so. Fight for me, Deirdreen!"

"Ardan, my dear brother," said Deirdre, "come to me and give me ten kisses."

"I'll miss my turn," he wailed, as he moved round to her.

They ate their supper, and were sitting

at chess—that is Deirdre and Naoise were
playing while the others watched the game,
when there came a tapping at the door
which was nearest to them.   Naoise held
a piece poised in his fingers.

"Go, Ainnle, and challenge that person."

"It is a woman's voice," said Ainnle.

"Let her come in."

The great bolts were pushed back, and
Lavarcham entered.

"My babe, my treasure!" she cried,
and she ran to Deirdre.

"Oh, my sweet mother!" said Deirdre.

"I have no time," Lavarcham panted.
"I must fly back to the king.   He sent me
to spy on you through the window."

"There is danger, mother?"

"There is terrible danger.   Conachúr's
household men are standing to arms in the
Speckled Branch, and there is a posse at
each of the gates of this place.   He will
attack before morning.   Oh, Deirdre,
Deirdre, that you could have come here
knowing Conachúr as I taught him to you!
What madness brought you from Scotland,
child?   Are you glad to see me?   Do you
love your mother still, little one?   I have

told the king that you would be ruined with hardship and sorrow; alas! you are more beautiful than ever. I shall tell him that you are one-eyed and lame, I shall tell him anything to quieten him for this night. To-morrow Naoise's people will get news of your return and he may fear to attack. If only I can quieten him for this night! He is drinking. He may go to sleep. Oh, my darling, my one love! I must fly. Keep all the doors barred. Do not open to any one. I shall send messengers to Uisneac's people. Kiss me again. Oh, my love of all loves! I must fly."

"Ainnle, Ardan, run round all the doors. See that they are secure," said Naoise.

He turned to Buinne and Iollann.

"Your father may be too late to help us. I give you back your protection, gentlemen."

"I shall stay with you," said Buinne.

"And I," said Iollann.

"Good comrades!" Naoise cried, and his eyes sparkled with delight and gratitude.

"We are five," he said, "trained to arms from the moment we could walk. No person of our quality will be against us, for no gentleman of Ireland would take part in such an attack. There will be only the common soldiery: hardy men, but as skilful at our trade as ploughmen. They cannot break in, for the Red Branch was designed not to be broken into. These bronze door——"

"The windows!" said Ainnle.

"God pity the man that gets in through a window," said Naoise. "Moreover, they are too high. A man's legs would be splintered if he jumped from them."

"Fire!" said Ardan.

"Conachúr will not burn his own fortress."

"There is a man at the window now," said Deirdre.

Naoise's hand was on the table. He picked up a heavy chessman of gold and ivory and with an underhand flick he sent it buzzing up and through the glass.

A roar of pain came from without and then a scream, "My eye! my eye!" a voice wailed.

"He won't peep through windows again in a hurry," said Ainnle.

"Conachúr has overreached himself," said Naoise. "We can hold out until the morning, and if Lavarcham sends her messages my people will be baying around Conachúr like wolves, and there will be many another one with them."

"The people of Fergus mac Roy will be with them," cried Buinne.

"That king will learn what it is to dare my father's protection," Iollann raged.

"Why," said Naoise joyfully, "we are as safe as if we were in Scotland."

"If we are only as safe as that!" said Ardan with a giggle. "Buinne, my soul, we used to be running from morning until night. We ate our food on the run. We used to run in our sleep. I tell the world that in six years I have not felt safe for a minute until this minute, for there are stout walls around us, and food to last a week's siege. The gods be praised," he said piously, "we cannot run even if we have to."

The band of young men shouted with laughter, and Deirdre chimed in as joyously as any of them.

CHAPTER XI

"IT is as you thought, master," said Lavarcham. "The girl is ruined."

"You saw her?"

"Her cheeks are hollow and her eyes are red. One would pity her, master. Indeed, I shall go to see her to-morrow."

"You did not want to see her any more," said the king.

"It was so," she replied humbly. "But my heart was wrung when I looked on her wretchedness."

"And the young men?"

"They are stout young men, master."

"And the guards that I posted?"

"They were at their posts."

"There ends a tale, and seven of my poor years . . .!" said Conachúr. "What did she look like, woman?"

232

"She is thin and haggard, and she leaned by the table as though all the weariness of the world were in her sides."

"Thus . . .!" said Conachúr. "And we fash ourselves for these things and spend our years and our pith . . .! Fill my cup, Lavarcham. Let the years go and the rest, for we are fools and children. Get to your rest, friend, and let me mourn my foolish years and all my nonsense."

"Nay, go to your bed also, sweet king," said Lavarcham. "You shall rest to-night, for that bad dream is ended. You will be troubled no more. To-morrow will be a new day, and all that the world has is for the king."

"It is so," said Conachúr. "This will be the last of those nights. Go to your bed, good soul, and I shall go to mine in a moment."

Lavarcham left the palace with her mind in a turmoil of weariness and fear, but with hope dawning in her soul. She sent secret runners to the men of Uisneac and to those of Fergus mac Roy, warning them that their chiefs were in urgent danger; and when she slept she was too happy even to remember what the king might do when he discovered her treachery.   That memory would be for the morrow.

But the king did not sleep.

"I shall wait the report of that guard," he said, "and then I will be able to sleep."

The guard came moaning and limping.

"What ails you, man?" said the astonished king.

"Naoise," the guard stammered.   "He has knocked out my eye."

He removed his hand from his face, and there was one eye there, and a bloody mess where the other should have been.

"Did I not tell you," the king stormed, "that they were murderous men?   Did you take no heed in your work?"

"It was the woman saw me," the guard stammered.   "She told the man, and before I could move he threw a chessman at me and knocked out my eye.   My leg is broken too, master, for I fell from the window."

"You will make a better herdsman than soldier," said the king harshly. "You are one-legged, one-eyed, and stupid. Go to your bed, and be careful that you do not cut your throat by taking off your boots. What did the woman look like?"

"What woman, majesty?"

"The woman I sent you to look at."

"She looked like the woman I saw in the crystal."

"I know she did. What did she look like, fool?"

"She looked like the most beautiful woman in the world."

Conachúr turned his great head and wide eyes on the soldier.

"Be careful how you report to me, guard. How did that woman look? Is she thin-faced? Is she pale and haggard and wretched?"

"She is not, majesty. She is red-lipped and sweet-eyed and delicious. She is the loveliest woman that moves in the world."

"Sit on that stool. Do not mind your eye for a moment. We shall mind it for you in a little time. Answer my questions. Did that woman look young or old?"

"She looked young as a bride."

"Are her cheeks thin?"

"They are not thin; they are round and rosy."

"Are her eyes red and sunken?"

"They are clear as sweet water, majesty; they are coloured—But for looking into them I should have got away, for, having looked, I could not but keep on looking until Naoise threw his chessman."

"You are muddled," said Conachúr sternly.

"I would give my other eye for another look at her," said the guard savagely.

Conachúr leaped furiously to his feet.

"You shall be cared for," he said. "Go to your bed. A doctor shall be sent to you. A comrade will help you along. . . . Ho, there!" he thundered. "Ho, there, the guards!"

CHAPTER XII

"What do you hear, Ardan?"

"Big feet, and a big lot of them."

"The doors are well secured?"

"Every bolt is drawn."

"And the door we arranged for is left with only one bolt shot?"

"Yes. It is a quick, well-oiled bolt. It will open and close again like lightning."

There came a loud command, and, in a moment, a thundering knock.

Naoise strode to the door.

"Who goes there?"

"The king's men."

"What do you want?"

"We want the woman who is with you."

"Is that all you want?"

"And we want Naoise, the son of Uis-neac."

"They are both here," said Naoise.

"Open this door," the voice commanded.

"Ah, no," Naoise laughed, "why should we do your business, honest man?"

There was no reply for a moment, but the rumble of conversation could be heard, then the voice came again.

"You others, Ainnle and Ardan and the sons of Fergus, open this door and you shall go free."

Naoise looked gravely at his companions.

"That is the necessary second part," said Buinne, hitching his sword-belt round.

Naoise's brothers took no notice, but their faces grew savage and their eyes narrowed and sparkled.

"Iollann and Deirdre, keep an eye on the windows," Naoise warned.

Iollann dangled a sling in his hand and Deirdre held another with a copper bolt in it.

"If," said the voice, "the woman Deirdre comes out we will go away."

"Watch the windows," Naoise warned; "they are talking to keep us occupied."

Deirdre's arm swung viciously, and a wild yell told that the bolt had gone home.

"I thought so," said Naoise. "They

238

cannot get in through the windows because
of the bars, but they could manage to fly an
arrow through, although it would be an
awkward shot."

"Why," said Ainnle, "we could go to
sleep here!"

A series of thundering knocks came on the
door.

"A ram!" said Buinne.

"Half-an-hour of that might bring even
these doors down," said Naoise.

He turned to his companions.

"Ardan, yours will be the first sortie.
They will not be prepared, lad, for it is very
awkward to work a ram and to keep guard
at the same time. Do not mind the men
with the ram; they will be unarmed. But
behind them there will be a mass of men.
You know how deep a fighter can penetrate!
It depends on his own weight. The instant
you touch that weight fight backwards.
When you are two yards from the door
Ainnle will shout. Turn then and run. I
shall have the door closed on you almost
before you are through. The moment the
door slams, you, Buinne, push in the bottom
bolt. I shall slide the middle one with my

239

right hand and will be reaching for the top one with my left. You are ready! Ardan, listen to me. The men immediately in front of you will give back a step until they start to come on. Fight, therefore, to the right, sidewards, and with the point all the time. Keep your left covered with the shield, and if there is a press cut with its cutting edges. The moon is high, and you will be able to see. No foolhardiness, boy! The moment you touch weight fight backwards, and then sweep broadly with the edge, and, when Ainnle shouts, run."

He turned again.

"Buinne, stand to the bolts. Iollann, Ainnle, Deirdre, place yourselves so, and sling the ramsmen or they may cumber his retreat."

Under the thundering batter of the ram and the savage roaring of the invaders the bolts were half drawn.

"Ready all!" said Naoise. "Ready, Ardan?"

Ardan hunched the shield to his left side and crouched, staring.

"Good boy!" said Naoise. "Now, Buinne—Pull!"

They heaved the great door wide and Ardan went through it like an arrow.

"Sling, children," said Naoise. "Keep me informed, Ainnle. I must stick behind the door."

"He is at them, and well in. . . . Ah!" said Ainnle, and he slung shrewdly. "He has forgotten to thrust and is cutting. My thanks, Iollann, for that bolt. His shield work is excellent, brother, but he will cut. There is his limit, if he knows it. He is fighting back, and now he is thrusting where he should use the sweeping blade for a retreat! That ramsman, Iollann! This one for me, and you, sister, for the crouching man. I shall shout now."

"Ardan!" he roared.

The boy dropped his combat as a dog drops a toad. In three seconds he was through the doorway, and in four the door had slammed.

Naoise towered long and lean over his young brother.

"Good lad!" he said. "Well done, Ardan!"

"I killed a million," said Ardan.

A savage, raging yell came from without.
"They will begin to warm to it now,"
said Naoise, "and we must keep them
occupied. It is your turn, Ainnle. Give
your sling to Ardan."

Ainnle whizzed at one window and Deirdre
at another. Two loud shouts were heard.

"Whether they are hit or not their skulls
are cracked by the fall," said Naoise, "but the
windows do not matter. Come to this door."

"Why cannot I go out?" said Buinne.

"You and I are the heaviest metal, my
heart, and when the real fighting commences
we shall have plenty to do. This is only a
little fun for the boys. Ainnle, listen carefully. You will slip out by this door, and
will run, and fight as you run. Range where
you please, but run always. In five minutes
—do not delay, Ainnle—make for yonder
door. This one will be shut, and the slings-
men will be inside that door to cover your
retreat. It is understood?"

Ainnle nodded, and made his blade whistle
through the air. He heaved the shield from
his back to his shoulder.

"The instant you are in, Ainnle, fly to this
door again, while we close the other behind

you. Open all the bolts but one; Buinne will help, and I and Iollann will dart out for five minutes. I wish to see what arrangements they are making."

"Are you protecting my brother?" said Buinne savagely.

"No, my heart, I am giving him a run and spying their dispositions."

"I claim this combat," said the rough young man.

"You shall have one immediately afterwards. You and I together will make the tour of this fortress, shoulder to shoulder, Buinne. Will not that content you?" Naoise laughed.

"I was beginning to feel lonely," said Buinne. "We shall have a pleasant run."

"Ten minutes for our run," said Naoise. "Ready, Ainnle?"

His brother nodded.

"Run straight out, thirty feet out if you can. Double then as you please. Remember the door you are to come in by, and do all the damage you can. If you are in difficulty give our call."

"I could not get into difficulty in five minutes," Ainnle smiled.

"Ready, Buinne? Pull!"

Ainnle sped out, and the door slammed on him like thunder.

The uproar without had been terrific, but now it redoubled, and at times a long scream topped the noise as spray tops a wave.

"We cannot see our brother," said Deirdre nervously.

"We know his work," Naoise replied. "He is as safe for five minutes as if he were in bed."

"Your combat, Naoise!" she breathed.

"It will be the easiest of them all. There will be a rough companion with me. Run all to the other door," he cried. "Iollann! Deirdre! Ardan! Your slings! The bolts, Buinne! Pull, my soul!"

Far out in the moonlight Ainnle was coursing like a deer. The moon flashed on his blade and on his shield. Men ran from him, and men ran to head him off, and into the middle of these he went diving like a fish. A band from the right came rushing for the open door.

"Out, Buinne, for ten seconds, and back when he is through."

Naoise and Buinne leaped out with whirling weapons. There was a clatter of shields, a medley of shouts and curses, and in ten seconds they were in again and the door was closed.

"You opened a minute too early," said Ainnle. "I was all right."

"You did some damage?"

"Not badly."

"You didn't kill as many as I did," said Ardan.

"Pooh!" Ainnle retorted. "No one could kill as many as you except Cúchulinn."

"Let us arrange the next sortie," said Naoise.

CHAPTER XIII

CONACHUR had come to the Red Branch, and a great roar of cheering greeted him. He strode to the captain of his troop.

"Well, my soul?"

"We have begun, majesty."

"How is it going?"

"Excellently," said the captain. "We have lost about forty men already."

Conachúr stared at him.

"How did that happen?"

"It happened because of the king's royal decision to lodge these men in a fortress."

"You have five hundred men here!"

"When they are all killed," said the captain sourly, "we can call out another five hundred."

"What is the difficulty?" his master growled.

"A fortress with six doors. They leap

in and out of these doors the way frogs leap
in a pool. While we are using the ram on
this door they make a sally by another door,
this door, any door—and they are the devil's
own fighters! We don't know where to
expect them, and any one of those within
is the equal of ten of our men in fighting,
and the superior of them all in tricks. I am
to have them out before morning—it is the
king's orders, but I don't know how it is to
be done."

"Ram all the doors," said Conachúr.

"I have but one ram. I can get others
to-morrow."

"To-morrow will be too late," said the
king furiously. "We shall have half Ulster
on our backs to-morrow."

"I want scaling ladders, grapnels," said
the officer angrily. "This work has been
thrown on us at a moment's notice and we
are not prepared for it. I can get them out
in a day, but not in a night."

"Attack a door with your ram," snarled
Conachúr, "and guard your other doors."

"I am doing that," said the captain, "and
my men, I fear, are beginning to love the
work."

He returned to his place, and in a few minutes the thud and batter of the ram was heard again. Conachúr strode there and watched the work with savage impatience. The captain returned and stood by him.

"You put good doors in the Red Branch, majesty," he said cheerfully, "an hour of that ramming will begin to make them quiver."

A shout arose, but it was multiplied from every side by the roaring soldiery, and one could not tell from which direction danger came.

"They have popped out somewhere," said the captain. "In about two minutes they will pop in again, somewhere—they know but we don't, and in those two minutes we will lose five men or twenty."

"Stick to the ram," Conachúr roared. "Keep at that door, my men."

A wild yelling came from the side and a burst of men came pell-mell round the corner. Weapons were striking everywhere and anywhere.

"Which are our men and which are theirs?" said the captain. "Ours don't know in this light which is friend and which is enemy. *They* know," he said bitterly, "but we are killing one another."

Two figures detached themselves in the moonlight. They were bounding like great cats, and wherever there was a mass they bounded into it, burst through it, and leaped on.

"Ho, Conachúr!" a voice called, "do you remember Naoise?"

"Ho, traitor king!" another boomed. "Do you remember Fergus?"

"It is Naoise and Buinne this time," said the captain.

The two figures leaped at the ramsmen. The ram was dropped, and the unarmed crew fled yelling. The door that was being battered opened and shut, and the two figures were gone.

"That's how it's done!" said the captain.

"Get to the ram!" Conachúr roared.

CHAPTER XIV

"THE king himself is there," said Naoise.

"Let us hunt him," cried Ardan in savage glee.

"He will move about," Naoise replied. "We would never know where he is, and we should only waste time. We have but to hold out until the morning, and we can do it with ease. Why!" he cried, "we have forgotten our days of travel; Fergus himself may be here to-morrow."

"He will travel day and night, and by chariot where we came on foot," said Iollann. "He may be here in the morning."

Naoise nodded joyfully.

"He will have choked whatever is in it out of Borach's throat long before this," Iollann continued, "and he will be an angry man."

"If he came, even alone," said Naoise, "that rabble would fly."

"They will fly before he comes," Ardan boasted, "for it's my turn to go out now, and I shall show them a trick or two."

"It's two by two now, babe," said Ainnle, "so we are going out together."

"That man," Ardan mourned, "is trying to cheat me of my fame. Fight for me, Deirdreen!   Back me up, Naoise!"

"Hark to them battering," said Iollann.

"How angry some people get," Ardan giggled.

"Let us make a full sortie," Buinne cried. "We five could eat those soldiers."

"One must be left for the door," Naoise replied.   "Ardan——"

"No door for me!" said Ardan violently.

"Ainnle," said Naoise, "our lives will depend on the doorman."

"I shall go out the next time all by myself," Ainnle bargained.

His brother nodded, while Ardan danced for joy.

"Pooh!" Ainnle gibed.   "He thinks he is Cúchulinn!"

Ardan squared up and began to shoulder him and to speak very roughly.

"And I am better than Cúchulinn," he concluded.

Ainnle seized his head and gave him three kisses.

"Little brother!" he said, "you are even better than I."

"You are a good brother," said Ardan. "I shall not divorce you," and he returned the three kisses.

"Are we ready all?" said Naoise. "Then let us arrange this sally."

"It shall be in two parties. Buinne and——" he halted for one moment, "Buinne and Ardan, Iollann and myself."

"You trust Ardan to me!" said Buinne shortly.

"Why not?" said Naoise.

Deirdre was staring at her husband with a fixed, white stare, and Naoise's throat went suddenly dry. He strode to her.

"What is it?" he murmured.

"I have no vision," she whispered. "I do not know."

"You still think——?"

"I know it," she said, "but I do not know when."

He closed his eyes and turned again.

"We go through this door. Once out, you turn to the left, Buinne, and I to the right and away each on a grand half circle. When we meet we form in line and charge back to this same door: six feet between each man for sword-play; Buinne and I on the outside."

"I shall be quite on the outside," said Buinne.

"As you will, friend," said Naoise. "Get to the bolts, Ainnle. You two will watch over each other?" he said, but it was at Buinne he looked.

"I shall bring him back," said the gruff man.

"If one of Buinne's hairs is touched," Ardan boasted, "I shall give him one of my own hairs instead of it."

"You are ready, Ainnle?"

"How shall I know when to open the door?" Ainnle roared.

"My wits are going!" said Naoise. "We shall fight in silence, and when you hear our battle-cry open the door at that instant."

253

"Wait!" said Buinne. "Heavier blades are wanted for this sortie. It should be two-handed work at the edge of a thirty-foot line, and the shields must be left behind."

"My wits are indeed going!" said Naoise.

"I shall bring him back," said Buinne. "I take him under my protection," he growled.

"You two," said Naoise, "keep your shields. Buinne and I take the great swords, and we leave our armour off for speed. The outside men must run twice as quick as the inside ones," he explained to Buinne.

Buinne nodded and began to unlace his battle-coats. Deirdre flew to help him, and she looked at him with such soft affection that the youth marvelled. Naoise was bending the great blade that he got from Manannan mac Lir, the God of the Sea.

"Now, Ainnle, the door! Buinne is out first, I second, Iollann and Ardan together. Ready! . . . Pull!"

They were gone.

Ainnle and Deirdre slammed the door, and he stood with his back leaning against

it, staring as it were inwardly, and listening
with every pore of his body. Deirdre threw
her arms about his neck.

"Oh Ainnle! dear Ainnle!"

"It is lonely here," he muttered.

Her head drooped on his breast.

"Do not faint, sister, the door has yet
to be opened, and you must help with the
bolts."

"Hear those clowns roaring!"

"If our own men would but shout once,"
she moaned.

"I should open the door immediately,"
he smiled, "and this noble combat would
have a stupid end."

"To-morrow will never come," she moaned.

"Do not make my teeth chatter," said
Ainnle.

"We must attend to the door," he
continued. "I shall draw the top bolt now.
Crouch down with your hands on the bottom
one, and, when the shout comes, draw it; I
will draw the middle one, and when I say,
'Pull,' drag with me on the door. It is
almost too heavy for one man to move, but
between us—and they will push from the
outside."

Deirdre crouched at his knees. A vast confusion of noise began to draw nigh.

"They are coming back," said Ainnle. "Draw your bolt now, sister, and take hold of the knob."

Above the infernal uproar there came the shout they knew.

"Pull!" he roared.

The door gave, a great push from without helped it, and the four leaped through. A blade leaped in behind them and was snapped in pieces as Ainnle, and a shoulder helping, smashed to the door.

Buinne was panting heavily.

"That deserves a rest," he said.

And the other three began with one voice to narrate the sortie to the two who had been within.

CHAPTER XV

BUINNE stood up.

"Naoise," he said sternly.

"My soul?" said Naoise.

"You interfered in my combat."

"Your end of the line was almost too heavy for any man, dear heart."

"You did it twice."

"Thirty feet out is a great distance. All the press was in your path. I did but lighten it when my own front was easy."

"I will accept no man's assistance," said Buinne.

"We are comrades," Naoise replied gently. "We give and take help."

"Did I call for help?" the other growled.

Naoise's great chest rose, but his voice was calm.

"No man will ever hear you call for help, Buinne."

"Let no man give what is not called for."

"But for that help, Buinne, you would now be dead."

"I was not fit for the end of the line?" said Buinne harshly.

"You are young yet, comrade, but in two years you will have the speed and smash that such a post calls for."

"Your speed! your smash!" said the sardonic Buinne.

"The world knows," Ainnle interposed, "that the four greatest champions of Ireland are Cúchulinn, Fergus, Conall, and Naoise."

"And Ainnle," Buinne completed with a grin.

The young man turned his dancing length of whipcord and his narrowed brow on Buinne.

"I, myself——" he said gently.

"And so could I," said Ardan.

"Do not quarrel," Naoise interrupted. "In two years Buinne will be the equal of any man you have named. Hush," he said.

He bent his head sideward and hearkened

in amazement.   The others listened, with
their eyes turned questioningly on each other.
They listened to nothing, for the ram had
ceased and there was a silence of the dead
without.

In a few moments there came a gentle
tapping, then a louder knocking at the door.

Naoise stood before it, frowning.

"Who goes there?"

"The herald."

"What do you want?"

"Parley."

"Say what you have to say, herald."

"If the woman Deirdre is put out through
this door the troops will march away."

"And what then?"

"No vengeance will be for ever exacted
against the sons of Uisneac."

"There is no answer," said Naoise.

"I have yet a message," said the voice.

"Deliver it."

"It is for the ear of the sons of Fergus."

Buinne strode forward.

"Deliver it," he said.

"There is no quarrel," said the herald,
"between the king and Fergus mac Roy.
The king's love for Fergus is such that he

wishes at any cost to save his two sons from
a death that is certain."

"Well?" said Buinne.

"The king says that if these young men
retire from the combat he will bestow a lordship on them."

"What lordship?"

"A cantred of land greater than that
which Fergus himself has, and the king's
friendship."

Buinne looked under steep red brows at
Naoise.

"I shall go out," he said.

He turned to his brother.

"You will come out with me."

"I shall not," said Iollann.

His brother stamped a foot.

"My father is my chief," said Iollann.
"What he orders I do. I cannot protect
the sons of Uisneac as he commanded, but
I can fight beside them."

Buinne turned.

"Herald," he roared, "tell Conachúr
that I shall go out to him."

His hand went to the door, but Naoise
stepped forward.

"Do not touch a bolt," he commanded.

"You shall go out by the door I choose. That door," he pointed, and strode to it. "Iollann, Ainnle, stand so with the spears, Ardan, Deirdre, sling from this point. Buinne stand so, one foot beyond the swing of the door."

"We may meet again, Naoise," said Buinne.

"If we meet in the press, Buinne, I may perhaps spare you for the sake of my brother Iollann. Ready, Buinne! When the door is opened I shall count three. Be gone ere the last count or I shall smash you to a pulp."

Naoise gave one mighty heave, and counted. Then Buinne was gone and the door had closed again.

"I claim this sortie," said Iollann, as the ram recommenced on the door.

"It is my turn," said Ainnle, "but we will go together, friend."

"I wish to go alone, and bring honour back to the name of Fergus. I am a better fighter than you think," he insisted.

"You are a good fighter in truth," said Naoise, "but a solitary venture is now dangerous. They are more accustomed to

261

the light and to our methods, for there is
nothing to vary in them. We must emerge
by a door, and they are watching every door
like hawks. But before you go, Iollann,
there is one work we must do for safety's
sake. Listen carefully, my dear ones."

CHAPTER XVI

" THIS is endless," Conachúr gritted. " Has
that Buinne come out yet?"

" The men will shout when he appears."

" Bring him here and we will get their
dispositions from him."

" There is nothing to get, majesty. Their
plan is the simplest. They have six
doors: they choose one to come out by
and one to get in by. That is the whole
plan."

" Post men in such a way that when
one does come out he will not be able to
get in again through that door or any door.
Send for reinforcements and put fifty men
against each door. . . . Those ramsmen have
women's shoulders," he growled. " They
would beat a mud wall down in a month."

" It must give shortly," said the captain,

"but there will be no entrance when the door is down."

"No?" said Conachúr.

"They will have the inside barricaded, and our men will not dare that narrow, black, impeded passage. We could leave an hundred dead in that doorway and be no farther."

"There is Buinne," the captain continued, as a shout came from the side.

"Buinne," said Conachúr, "you will fight for me?"

"My lordship, Conachúr?" said the gruff young man.

"It shall be as I said, and more," said the king. (It was given as promised, and was known for long as Dal Buinne, but it is now called Slieve Fuad.)

Buinne told what he could of the defence, but, as the captain had foreseen, there was nothing to tell.

"This door," said Conachúr, "will be down shortly. Have they barricaded it on the inside?"

"They have not," said Buinne.

The captain became active and violent.

"Ah!" he cried, "there is always something forgotten."

"Get at the ram, you there," he roared. "Put your shoulders into it."

He turned to the king.

"We have them!" he said.

Conachúr, with his eyes gleaming and a savage smile curling his lips, strode towards the rammers, but as he moved the door swung open and four men leaped from its yawning blackness. In a second two of the ramsmen were dead, and the rest were flying wildly, bustling the very king in their passage.

"By my hand!" the captain gurgled.

Two of the assaulters lifted the ram and trotted with it through the door. The other two made an onslaught of such ferocity that the soldiers were appalled. Then one fled back through the door, which instantly slammed, and the other sped like lightning around the building.

"After him!" roared Conachúr.

But the captain remained where he was, howling and dancing with rage.

"I've lost my ram," he bawled. "I've lost my ram."

265

"We have you, Iollann!" said Conachúr.
"Traitor to your king!" he growled.

"Traitor to your friends," Iollann retorted.

"Deliver yourself to me," said Conachúr,
"and you shall be spared."

"I came out for a purpose," said Iollann.
"I demand single combat."

"There are no gentlemen here," Conachúr replied, "except your brother, so your
claim cannot be granted."

"I shall cuff him," said Buinne, "but I
will not fight him," and he strode away.

"I shall take this combat," said a voice.

Conachúr turned and saw his own son,
Fiachra, standing there, and his heart
sank.

"You have no arms," he said harshly.

"You will lend me yours," said Fiachra.

Conachúr stared on the fierce circle that
surrounded him. He stared at Iollann,
who stood with his back to the Red Branch
swinging his blade, and he knew that the
combat must take place.

"Iollann and I were born on the same
night," said Fiachra. "It is an equal
combat."

Conachúr took off his own battle-coats and gave them to Fiachra. He gave him his shield, the enchanted Aicean, and his green sword.

"Fight, then," he said, "and remember my teaching. Remember my shield work and my thrust."

They fought then, but at the first stroke from Iollann the great shield roared; for that virtue was in the Bright-Rim, to roar when the man it covered was struck at, and in answer to its roar the Three Waves of Ireland, the Wave of Tua, the Wave of Clíona, and the Wave of Rury roared in reply, and thereby all Ireland knew that a king was in danger.

Away in the palace Conall Cearnach sat drinking, listening to some great brawl, as he thought. He heard the roaring of Aicean, and leaped to his feet.

"The king is in danger!" he said.

He seized his weapons and fled from the palace of Macha, and came on the great combat.

In the dim light he thought it was Conachúr himself was behind the shield, and from

267

the daring and mighty onslaught of the opponent he saw there was no time to lose. He burst his blue-green spear through the press and through the back of Iollann.

Iollann staggered to the wall of the Red Branch.

"Who has struck me from behind?" he said.

"I, Conall Cearnach."

"Great and horrible is the deed you have done, Conall."

"Who are you?" Conall demanded.

"I am Iollann the Fair, sent by my father to protect the sons of Uisneac."

"By my hand," said Conall fiercely, "I shall undo some of what I have done," and with one side twist of the sword he lifted the head from Fiachra.

"Help me to that door, Conall," said Iollann. "The sons of Uisneac are within."

The appalled soldiery shrank back, and on Conall's arm they came to the door. There Iollann gave his shout. A feeble one it was, but it was heard and the door opened. Iollann staggered in.

"Fight bravely, Naoise!" he said, and

with that he sank on the floor, and he was dead.

Outside the Red Branch Conachúr ran hither and thither like a man enraged by madness.

CHAPTER XVII

"WE are yet three," said Naoise. "Draw
the bolts, Ainnle, for one sortie of friendship. We have no doorman, for Deirdre
could not close or open the door by herself.
You and I, Ainnle. Be quiet, Ardan!
Come, my brother, and put all your arm
into the blade. We will come in by the
door we go out of. This door! Be ready
for our shout, Ardan!"

They went out and returned with red
weapons, and for a long time they sat in
the dim flare of a torch watching by their
dead comrade.

"He was a brave boy," said Deirdre.

"He did not obey my order," her husband
sighed. "I do not know what he did."

"I smell—smoke," said Ainnle suddenly.

"I have smelled something for a long

time," said Deirdre, "but I could not think
what it was. I am weary because of the
death of this good friend."

But little by little the vast building
became full of smoke, and in a while a fierce
roar and crackling was heard also.

Naoise was again the hardy leader.

"They have fired the fortress! We do
not know what happened while Iollann was
away, but Conachúr has reached the end of
the world. Who could have foretold that
he would fire the Red Branch! We must
prepare for all that can happen."

"We are not dead yet," said Ardan.

"What do you counsel, brother?" said
Ainnle.

"Sit down, there is less smoke on the
floor."

A ruddy glare could be seen by each
window.

"Fire is laid all round the building. We
must make our plans quickly."

Ainnle turned gleefully to his younger
brother.

"You shall run after all, my poor friend."

"In good truth," Ardan grinned, "I
thought in Scotland that I should never

want to run again, but I feel now that we have been staying too long in the one place. After all," he said complacently, "I am a man of action."

"And, of course," Ainnle gibed, "no one can run as quickly as you can."

"No one," said Ardan, "except Deirdre."

"Listen," said Naoise. "We have still more than a chance. We can run. Scotland trained us in that certainly, and if we can surprise but forty yards on the men without, we will outrun their best in twenty minutes."

"Where shall we run to?"

"We shall take the road to our own lordship. If Lavarcham's message has been sent our kinsmen should be marching at this moment on Emain. But," he said, and pointed, "we cannot wait for them."

They looked in silence.

A huge, golden flame licked screaming through the window, wavered hither and thither like some blindly savage tongue, and roared out again.

"It was ten feet long and three feet thick," said Ardan in a whisper.

"In ten minutes we will go," said Naoise.

"What arms?"

"Shield and spear, brother. Strip off all armour. We must run lightly."

"I shall be out first," he continued. "Give me twenty seconds before you follow, Ainnle, I can make room in twenty seconds. You will run ten paces to the left of the door. Deirdre and Ardan will run immediately into our interval; turn all to the right, and at my shout, run. Single file; Ainnle at the end. If I shout 'halt,' you two turn about and protect the rear. When I shout 'run,' drop every combat and fly. You, Deirdre, take Iollann's shield."

"And his spear," said Deirdre.

"Keep actually at my back, beloved, and each time we halt drop flat on the ground."

He was shouting his instructions now, for the voice of the fire was like the steady rage and roar of the sea, and through every window monstrous sheets of flame were leaping and crashing.

"This door," said Naoise. "A kiss for every one," he called. "We shall win yet. Pull, Ainnle!"

"The door is red hot," said Ainnle.

"Back for a mantle; two. Now grip. Pull! Give me twenty seconds, Ainnle."

He leaped across fire and disappeared.

The others leaped after him, with a wild yell from Ardan.

Conachúr had sent a flying messenger to the palace.

"Bring Cathfa back with you," he ordered. "Tell him I want him. Say that the king beseeches him to come."

The captain of his troop stood by.

"Alas for the Red Branch!" he said mournfully.

"All that can be destroyed can be rebuilt," said Conachúr. "I shall rebuild the Red Branch."

He was in terrible distress and agitation.

"The morn is nigh," he said.

And he strode unhappily to and fro, with his eyes on the ground and his mind warring.

Far to the east a livid gleam appeared. The darkness of a summer night, which is yet a twilight, was shorn of its soft beauty, and in the air there moved imperceptibly and voluminously a spectral apparition of dawn. A harsh, grey, iron-bound upper-

world brooded on a chill and wrinkled earth.
The king's eyes and the eyes of his captain
scanned each other from colourless, bleak
faces. There was no hue in their garments;
their shields were dull as death; and their
hands, each clutching a weapon, seemed like
the knotted claws of goblins.

A slow, sad exhalation came from the
king's grey lips, like the plaint of some
grim merman of the sea, rising away and
alone amid the chop and shudder of his
dismal waters.

"The fire is catching," the captain murmured. "Hark to that crackling!"

"We shall have light," the king murmured.
"The Red Branch will flame."

"Within . . .!" said the captain moodily,
and he looked with stern mournfulness on
the vast pile.

"They must soon come out," he muttered.

"Your men are posted?"

"Every door is held. When they pop
out this time——"

"They will have no place to pop into,"
said Conachúr. "I have them," he growled;
and he threw his hand in the air and gripped

it, as though in that blanched fist he held all that could never escape from him.

"They will fight," said the captain, "and they are woeful fighters."

"You are nervous, man," said Conachúr.

"At this hour and after this night," said the captain, "our men could fly from those three like scared rabbits."

"I fear that," said Conachúr.

"They may get away," said the captain.

Conachúr advanced on him so savagely and with such a writhe of feature that the man fell back.

"Dog!" said Conachúr. "If they escape I shall take your head."

"They are surrounded," the captain stammered; "they cannot escape."

"They can escape," Conachúr roared. "You know they can escape. Your men are cowards and idiots, and what are you? Oh, am I not a thwarted man! Am I not a forsaken king! Where is Cathfa? Where is the druid?" he cried.

"Majesty," the captain implored, "do not curse us. The great magician is coming."

The magician indeed had come.

"What has set you raging, Conachúr?" he asked.

"Father," said Conachúr. "If you do not assist me I am lost."

The old, old man looked at him.

"Tell me your tale, son. Whom have you locked up in fire?"

"The sons of Uisneac are there," said Conachúr. "They will escape me," he said.

"They are my grandchildren," said Cathfa.

"It is the woman with them. It is Deirdre I want. She was mine. She was stolen from me. I am not myself without her. I am a dead man while she is with Naoise."

"What do you fear from boys roared round by flame?"

"They may escape with her. When they come out my men may run from them. If they escape this time, father, I am dead."

"If I help you, Conachúr——!"

"I shall do anything you ask. Nothing you can demand will be too much for Conachúr."

"It is the woman you want?"

"The woman only."

"It is not the blood of these boys you lust for?"

"The woman, father, only the woman."

"I shall help you, Conachúr. Do not lay one finger on my daughter's sons, the sons of your young sister."

"They are out," the captain said, as a great roar came from the soldiers.

Conachúr moved to that direction.

"Quick, quick," he said, twitching his father's mantle in his impatience. "They will escape me."

"They shall not escape me," Cathfa answered. "There is no need for haste."

They were out, indeed, and, like two grim lions or woeful griffins of the air Naoise and Ainnle were raging in that press. Into their interval leaped Ardan, with but one eye peeping from the shield and a deadly hand thrusting from the rim. Back and forth they leaped with resistless savagery. Men flew at them and from them. Everywhere was a wild yelling of orders and the

278

wilder screaming of stricken men. But over all Naoise's voice came pealing—

"Up, Deirdre. Run!"

She was at his back in an instant: the shield covering her side, her spear darting viciously by his right elbow, and a venturesome man dropped squealing. Five feet behind Ardan was leaping like a cat, all eyes and points, and ten paces behind him Ainnle was bounding.

"Halt," roared Naoise.

Deirdre was again on the ground. Ardan ranged tigerishly to right and left, while Ainnle whirled on the pursuers in ten-foot bounds.

Conachúr had arrived with Cathfa. Men were falling before them at the rate of three a second. So dreadful was Naoise's onslaught in the front that none would face him. Men tumbled over each other when he charged.

"The men will run away in a second," said the captain.

"Get into the *mêlée*, coward," roared Conachúr. . . . "Cathfa——!" he implored.

279

The officer whizzed out his blade and leaped forward. In three seconds he was dead, and five who followed him were rolling in their agony along the ground.

Naoise's voice came in a wild shout.

"Up, Deirdre. Run!"

The four were again in line. The men in front melted to either side of that dreadful file.

"Run!" said Naoise. "We are out!"

In front of him there was but Conachúr and Cathfa. Conachúr drew his great sword and stood crouching; and at him, with a dreadful smile, Naoise came on. Cathfa moved two paces to the front and stared fixedly at Naoise. He extended his two arms widely——

Naoise dropped on one knee, rose again, leaped high in the air and dropped again on his knee. Deirdre fell to the ground and rose up gasping. Ardan rolled over on his back, tossed his shield away, and came slowly up again, beating the air with his hands. Ainnle went half way down, rose again, and continued his advance on tiptoe.

A look of dismay and rage came on Naoise's face. He moved with extraordinary slowness to Deirdre and lifted her to his shoulder.

"We are lost," he said. "That magician——!"

"Keep on swimming," Ardan giggled. "There was never water here before, but the whole sea has risen around our legs, and we may paddle to Uisneac."

The arms dropped from their hands, and, in fact, they swam.

Not for a minute or two did the soldiers dare advance, and then they did so cautiously. They picked up the fallen weapons, and then only did they lay hands on the raging champions.

Cathfa dropped his arms to his sides.

"We are taken," said Naoise. "Our run is ended."

CHAPTER XVIII

CATHFA had gone away, and Conachúr strode to his prisoners.

"So! Naoise," he said.

"So! uncle," said Naoise.

"I win in the end. I always win at last," said Conachúr.

He looked at each with his stern smile, and when he spoke again it was to Deirdre.

"Little fawn! you have run wild for a long time. You shall rest at last."

But she made only the reply that a fawn makes, the reply of parted lips and terror-stricken eyes.

"You shall come to me," he said.

Then she moistened her trembling lips and looked at Naoise.

"Do not look at him," said Conachúr.

"He is already a dead man; let him be forgotten. All tricks and troubles are ended for you, sweet bird; you shall have peace."

"Will you have peace to-morrow, Conachúr?" said Naoise. "Fergus is marching on you."

"Be at ease, nephew," and the king smiled grimly. "I shall take care of Fergus when he comes. For long I have wanted to take care of Fergus. But, first, I shall take care of you, Naoise, and of your traitor brothers. Your hour is on you," he said, "and you die now."

"Churl and rogue——!" said Ainnle.

But a gesture from his brother stopped him.

"Let this king do his business," he said.

"That must be done," said Conachúr.

He turned briskly and moved away.

Now the day was at hand, and these four looked on a world that was spectral and misshapen, but which was yet the world. On high the clouds could be seen, a grey immensity, stony as the face of Conachúr, and a chill wind moaned thinly about them. But far away the grey misery of morn had lightened, and a silver gleam, slender as a rod, crept up the east.

To that gleam their eyes turned, and from it to each other's faces.

At the guards who ringed them in they did not look, or they looked unseeingly. But those gaunt apparitions stared like statues on the four and did not move a lip.

"The sun will rise in a little," said Ardan. . . . "That magician has gone," he whispered. "If we leaped at the guards——!"

"No good, brother, they are too many and we have no arms."

"We should have one merry minute," said Ardan.

"We have had a merry night," said Ainnle, "be contented, babe."

Naoise looked lovingly on his brothers.

"We were always together," he said. "We shall always be together."

"And I . . . !" said Deirdre, "am I to be left out at last?"

"Sweet girl," said Naoise; "he will kill

us, but you will be spared. You shall
see that sun come up. You shall look at it
for us."

"Dear husband," she said, "do you still
love me? Do you truly love me?"

His eyes gave her answer.

"Here comes Conachúr," said Ainnle.

"And a large person with him," said
Ardan.

It was Mainè Rough-Hand, son of the
King of the Fair Norwegians, they say; but
others think it was Eogan, son of Durthacht,
the prince of Ferney.

"You shall die at the hand of a gentleman
as befits your rank," said Conachúr.

"I shall be the first," said Ardan briskly.
"I am first in every great deed," he explained to Conachúr.

"Hark to him!" Ainnle laughed.
"Respect your elders, young person, and
the heads of your family."

But Ardan appealed to Mainè.

"Let me be first, sweet sir," he pleaded.
He turned confidingly to Conachúr. "I
cannot bear to see my brothers killed," he
said. . . .

Deirdre knelt by the bodies, and she sang their keen, beginning:

"I send a blessing eastward to Scotland."

When she had finished the poem she bowed over her husband's body: she sipped of his blood, and she died there upon his body.

SO FAR, THE FATE OF THE SONS OF UISNEAC, AND THE OPENING OF THE GREAT TAIN